JUST OUT OF YOUR GROUND

I0144980

Also by Bill Reed

novels
Dogod
The Pipwink Papers\
Me, the Old Man
Stigmata
Ihe
Crooks
Tusk
Throw her back
Are You Human?
Awash
Tasker Tusker Tasker
Lankan 1001 Nights Book 1
Lankan 1001 Nights Book 2
White Wi
nonfiction
Water Workout
staged and published plays
Burke's Company
Truganinni
The Pecking Order
Mr Siggie Morrison and Comb and Paper
Jack Charles is Up and Fighting
Just Out of Your Ground*
You Want It, Don't You, Billy?
I Don't Know What to Do with You.
Paddlesteamer
Cass Butcher Bunting
Bullsh
More Bullsh
Talking to a Mirror
Mirror, Mirror
Auntie and the Girl
Daddy the 8th
Truganinni Inside Out
Living on Mars
Living in Black Holes
Shorts
The modern shadow plays
Nosey Parker
Dimmer
Tears and the Tail Light
Top Knot Down
Banana Split
Tanzir's Fifth
award-winning short stories
Messman on the C.E. Altar
English Expression
The 200-year Old Feet
The Case Inside
Blind Freddie Among the Pickle Jars
The Old Ex-serviceman
Mahood on the Thin Beach
The Shades of You my Dandenong

JUST OUT OF YOUR GROUND

(or, the floundering of W.A.)

Bill Reed

R

First published by Reed Independent, Melbourne, Australia 2017

Printed by CreateSpace, an Amazon.com company

Available from Amazon.com, CreateSpace.com, Kindle estores, and also from most other major book retail chains and online retail outlets worldwide as:
9780995395763 (paperback)
9780995395770 (ebook)

National Library of Australia Cataloguing-in-Publication entry:
Author: Reed, Bill
Title: Just Out of Your Ground
ISBN: 9780995395763 (paperback)
             9780995395770 (ebook)
Subjects: Peel, Thomas, 1793-1865
             Swan River Colony
             Western Australia
Dewey No.:   821.33

Dedication

for Gill Mennell and the sharing of her keepsakes

First Showings

Prior to this 2017 rewrite which itself followed years of the original script being lost, JUST OUT OF YOUR GROUND was first performed in January 1975 by the then-Monash Student Theatre for its Victorian tour and for a season back at Alexander Theatre, Monash University.

The cast consisted of: Don Smith, Peter Gerrard, Jill Mennell, John Maddick, Chris Dobney, Margaret Noyle, Margaret Gott, Richard Tulloch. The director was Andrew Ross.

The Characters

THOMAS PEEL
Aristocratic leader of the first organized settlement; a klutz at organizing; a clutcher at straws. Hardly able to get off the beach – struck dead-stuck, emotionally and physically. As alive as, yes, a piano. Deserted by friend, relative and foe alike, save for his mother-in-law of nearly 30 years, if he ever dared count, which he didn't. and just had to lampoon himself towards the end by finally reaching out… and what happened?; he groped the wrong thing. Poor 12th man, he just got caught out of his ground.

MRS AYRTON
His mother-in-law, and a classic one at that. She would not be for gagging and bounding that which cried out for gagging and bounding. Her own woman, since no one seemed to be inclined to make it otherwise. Had ample resources behind her, which were, in terms of being shown before the assizes, tangible – and so, finally, had Peel caught in a grope that would make you gasp.

MOCK
(nickname for MOKKARA), an Aboriginal manservant bequeathed to Peel back in the motherland. Taken to England from New South Wales in earliest colonial days for 'tickle-the-specimen' purposes. This was right; he was a specimen – a specimen of a superiorly intelligent human being. He was never ever going to live in livery. A smile on his lips that had every right to turn into a smirk, but didn't because he would make sure it never needed to.

FRED PEEL
Peel's 'son', but openly known as the love-child of Mrs Peel,

3

and one who knows his place is at the foot – under – of his 'father'. The colony gives him the expanses of inner space which, in turn, allows him greater roles than playing the dutiful son. But keeps the 'dutiful' part and that's the thing.

MACQUEEN
Lieutenant in rank and in law-and-order very rank. In legal matters, full of handcuffs; with Peel's wife, hands cuff; with Peel, cuff-hands paddy-whack. Spiffing when it was worth the spit, and a spitter when he thought it might be spiffing. Doesn't know when he's cuckolding or the cuckold; never bothered with what it meant anyhow, what?

MRS PEEL
Married to Peel young and never forgot not to get over it. Has the wifely tones of 'oh dear', though, which husbands never take notice of. Peel most certainly was no exception. With her wandering eye and mind, a natural as an early settler, being an explorer of the males around her by inclination, especially if the next man invited her over the next sand hill. One day might reach the limits of her bed.

DORA PEEL
Daughter, who might still be asleep if she hadn't woken up and discovered she was of age, then gone back to sleep to get over it. HALL was made to suffer there.

HALL
Stable master/hand of Peel and swain of DORA. Swaps his saddles for a robe and, in so doing, hands the shovel to clean any future stable floors over to Peel, right smartly and with lip-smacking relish.

ACT 1

1.

(Through the darkness, there are the sounds of a raging storm at sea – driving rain, breaking waves, thunder and lightning.

There are also the fearful sounds of a ship perhaps breaking up or at least under great stress, with raucous shouting from the crew and passengers.

Halfway through this maelstrom, a light in the mid sky starts to intensify and then is shown to be coming from a big and bright sun. It evokes a brilliant and clear day in contrast to the chaos of the storm and from the arrival of the ship, even while the sights and sounds of climate and human chaos continue 'around' it.

During a long moment, the feeling of overall turbulence ceases. There is only this strange clear-sky light beginning to flood the stage – again, this is quite separate from the strange unerring calm-centric sun. For this time, all is stillness... a promise of a new day, a new beginning.

Then the sounds of the storm and the near-wrecking of the ship gradually return and become dominant. By the human cries, the survivors and stores are being loaded into lifeboats. These reach a frenzy and a crescendo, before abruptly cutting off again.

Pause.

Within the re-flooding light of the strange and central

*sun… blinded by its intensity… comes PEEL, stumbling
(but remaining stoically upright) into it. He stands
'within' its glare.*

*He is standing on an upright piano which has already
sunk up to the top of its legs in the sand. It looks
cemented in place… and metaphorically is.*

*We can now better see how he is dressed ridiculously
formally for the situation he is in – in breeches and
boots and waistcoat and jacket, with pinned cravat,
carrying a half-top hat.*

*He stands stoically as a true blue-blooded aristocrat at
the time would, as if he was still surveying his manor in
England. He is not in England. He is in a wasteland of
a beach on the other side of the world from that.*

*But he seems totally unmindful of that. It seems his only
concern is to stare down… to even wear down… the
peculiar unerring sun that seems to be obsessing him,
with his sheer presence, and not just of mind. While
there are intimations of much movement on the beach
all around him, he takes no notice of those. Instead he
continues to stare unblinkingly up at 'his' sun. He
doesn't even avert his challenging gaze to:)*

PEEL: Strange. Passing strange. No. Unpassing strange. A
bit… bloody queer. I am aware that at another time I might be
quoted. Bit of a pity.   ·

*(Slowly, as though 'his' sun itself is giving in to him, the
overall lighting becomes 'stage-wide', even while its
direct burning light remains the dominant feature
throughout.*

*Finally, MRS AYRTON comes, both with a harridan's
voice and a presumption that distracts even PEEL)*

MRS AYRTON: You know what I think, don't you? I think
you deliberately tipped me out. What more could be expected
of you? Certainly, not from yours truly. Me drowning with a
lung full of water from some strange foot I've only just put a
person on! You! You're going to get yours, Thomas Peel,
mark me.

PEEL: (barely deigning to answer) Get my what?

MRS AYRTON: How do I know what? I've only just set
foot on the place. Whatever it is, you're going to get it! You
should open your ears, or what's the use of a gal talking to
you?

PEEL: The last time you were a gal, my ears hadn't started
developing.

MRS AYRTON: Those ears of yours were born two hundred
years before you were!

PEEL: Well, they would've been around when you were
born. Just.

MRS AYRTON: I'm not taking any more insults you think
you're free to throw out here, either!

*(She bustles around 'settling' the few personal things, in
the manner of 'making' house – which additionally
annoys him -- until she cannot hold back:)*

MRS AYRTON: That was uncharted waters, that there was!
'Couldn't be found on any chart'… you think that's funny you
saying should go on my headstone?

PEEL: (mutters) No, but the headstone would be fun.

MRS ARYTON: Murderer! Don't think you're going to get away with it! I've got witnesses of you throwing your leg over the side and trying to put your foot in my mouth. Well, my mouth showed you!
    (and, whine)
My own daughter had to untie me from that brutish bit of iron you said was a life buoy. Half of my fingernails sank without trace down to the quick, did you ever think about that? Murderer! Perversion! Looker!

PEEL: (this stops him) What'd you say?

MRS AYRTON: Looker! Looker!

(PEEL bellows with rage, launches himself at her.

But she is obviously used to this, the way she wards off his initial lunge and how she then skirts around him to run off. He follows close behind. Just off stage, he obviously catches her.

We hear her screeching for help and the two of them struggling. He drags her back in, finally manages to gag her. It at least tones down her abuse to a muffle.

PEEL returns to on top of the piano. On an afterthought, he goes to just past one end of the instrument and pushes cricket stumps into the sand, as though the piano was part of a cricket pitch. He marks out the crease in the sand-dust on the piano, then, most importantly for him, returns to centre-piano and commences staring defiantly at 'his' unerring sun.

He and MRS AYRTON remains static while the lighting indicates a new day beginning, although for a moment the darkness around the edges surges forward before stopping and retreating. 'His' unerring sun, though, hasn't even blinked.

Blackout)

2.

(General lighting up on a new day.

From the centre of the piano, PEEL is continuing to stare up and challenge 'his' sun, even though the general lighting intimations are dawn time.

He is now surrounded by his inner circle. These are: MRS PEEL and her daughter DORA; his Aboriginal servant MOCK 'gifted' to him in England; FRED PEEL, HALL, MACQUEEN, besides MRS AYRTON, now recently unbound with the gag still slipped to being around her neck and one end of the 'tie' still tied around one wrist.

Apart from a still-alert(ed) PEEL, they are all in various positions of apparent well-earnt rests. Some are still asleep; others are waking up, mainly by slapping at the increasingly biting sand flies coming up with the sun. Apart from the fastidious dressiness of PEEL, they are all dressed shabbily... even in tatters. The ordeals of a rough landing and material losses are all too obvious.

Mainly through the agency of the annoying sand flies, PEEL relents staring defiance at 'his' sun and half stretches back onto the piano top, which has now sunk as low as it can go while still being recognizable.

*It is obviously his island upon which none can venture.
On it are: decanter and one port glass; handsome plate
enough for one; china cup and saucer and one teapot; a
china jug set for washing; a gentleman's pigskin
travelling valise still dripping sea water.*

*PEEL tries to stare his mother-in-law down, but few
humans could be that successful. He turns his imperious
eye onto the waking others and watches with
considerable distaste as MOCK, HALL and LT
MACQUEEN slap themselves awake from the sand flies.*

*He watches with further disdain as LT MACQUEEN
crawls over to rather improperly cover MRS PEEL with
his coat, and nods paternally when DORA comes awake
and looks to her father for re-assurance things are in
hand.*

*He turns his attention to FRED PEEL, lying literally at
his feet, and shows even greater disgust that the love-
child of his wife has the impertinence of sleeping with
his head on the piano key board. He kicks it off.*

*Though they are all awake now, none bother to rise
fully, but remain seated looking towards PEEL as to
what to do next.*

*PEEL is aware he has their attention but takes no
notice. Instead he takes up a snuff box, indulges in a
mighty pinch. He is about to smile to the snuff-full
world when he is bitten viciously by a sand fly, which he
slaps at but only hits himself in the back of the neck.)*

MACQUEEN: Gad a fly, sir!

FRED PEEL: (encouraged) A gaddle of a fly, father!

PEEL: Don't you two start.

(Thinking he has come alive and happily so, they start to babble among themselves until he stares them each down from 'atop' his piano. They quieten expectantly around him again, whenupon he vents his rage against FRED PEEL by stomping on him with each boot.)

PEEL: (in cadence with the blows) Let these be the first civilized acts in this colony.

(He then crosses the piano top to its 'wicket' end and, with the side of his foot, marks out a crease line in the sand gathered there, and:)

PEEL: Let this be the first mark of civilization.

MACQUEEN: It deserves to be the first!

PEEL: It does indeed! Anyone seen my bat?

MOCK: (indicating MRS PEEL) Right here.

PEEL: That'll be enough out of you, Mock. Have you run my bath?

MOCK: Can't find the bath, but found the runs, mighty sir.

MRS PEEL: Thomas!

PEEL: What, what?

MRS PEEL: (re her son FRED) You might have hurt his

feelings.

PEEL: I certainly hurt my boot. Next, you'll start going on again about no part of me has ever claimed him. This 'ere boot says otherwise.
   (then rounds on all)
And, pray, what are we all sitting around for?
   (they stare dumbly)
Go! Disperse! Spread thinly! Colonise! Do I have to do everything around here?

MACQUEEN: (rousingly) By gad, no!

PEEL: By God, there's another gad!

   (But their enthusiasm is dampened by MRS PEEL not letting the subject of her love child alone:)

MRS PEEL: He loves you like the father he never had!

PEEL: And I love him like his father not admitting he was his, not even when we strung him up. I won't mention sticking me with him being his real crime.

MRS PEEL: It wasn't little Fred's fault!

PEEL: That bough of that tree came cracking down. That was a perfectly good oak before his lot swung from it. Bad form, that.

FRED PEEL: (trying to be helpful, holding it up from underneath him) Found your bat, Father.

PEEL: Oh, it's 'father' now, is it?

FRED PEEL: Yes, Father.

PEEL: Nothing father from the damn truth.

MRS PEEL: Thomas!

PEEL: (mimic) 'Thomas!'

(PEEL snatches the bat away from FRED, dusts it off by clapping it up and down on FRED's shoulder, then... at last something shows promise!... practises forward movements from the crease, regardless of the looks all the others are throwing at each other.)

PEEL: (stopping to grandiose) I told the parliamentary committee that I would try to avoid nicking off the shoulder.

(There is no answer to this, except to start drifting away.)

MOCK: 'Ere, mighty sir, what're you gonna do?

PEEL: Hmm?

MOCK: There's this storm brewing.

PEEL: No storm.

MOCK: A storm, see.

PEEL: Nope.

MOCK: Rained off, like.

(This makes PEEL stop and think. He looks up at 'his' sun and then over to the darkness of the interior land-side, refers to MOCK to no one in particular:)

PEEL: Did this man hit his head again last night? Has anyone bothered to set up a sick bay? Can't get good helpers these days. Does anyone think we can be regarded as ship-wreck survivors or are we in muddy waters here?

MACQUEEN: (turning from MRS PEEL) Might there be an additional government subsidy coming for that? Muddy waters not specified in the contract?

PEEL: I think you should look that up, Lieutenant Macqueen.

MACQUEEN: I think you should look it up, sir.

PEEL: Hardly.

MACQUEEN: I concur.

PEEL: So we'll leave it to you to look it up, shall we?

MACQUEEN: Hardly, old chap.

    (He has confused even himself)

MOCK: (getting fed up) Mighty sir, these blessed sand flies are driving me loony, an' that's a fact. Can we get off here?

PEEL: They're your blessed flies, Mock.

MOCK: Mighty sir, don't Mock me.

PEEL: I am not mocking you, Mock.

MOCK: Seems you be.

PEEL: Doesn't don't.

MOCK: Does so.

PEEL: Why does this fellow keep arguing with his betters? I can never say a word.

MOCK: Keeps me English learning, mighty sir.

PEEL: (correcting) 'Keeps me learning English'.

MOCK: ('ergo') There, working already, mighty sir.

(But his earlier beginnings of scratching at the midge bites gets the better of him. He scratches more, then gives way to a bout of frenzied scratching.

It affects the others. One by one, they begin to scratch themselves and then also to give in to the momentary pleasure of frantic attacking the itches.

Even PEEL begins to squirm as, in added turn, he watches them succumb one by one, until:)

PEEL: No scratching!

(They try their best… behind his back… to obey)

PEEL: That is the order of the day.

(They all manage to stop, but they can't stop their fingers from trying to get back to the bites.

There is a lot of surreptitious rubbing of backs against each other, etc, until it is PEEL himself who cannot stand it any longer. He gives in and 'gets' at the middle of his back with his bat, cries out with relief…)

15

PEEL: Ooooo…

> *(It is a signal for all to give sway to bouts of tearing at their bites. There is a long moment when not one of them can even look up from the hot pleasure they are giving themselves, until MACQUEEN seems to notice some movement in the dark interior around them)*

MACQUEEN: I say, did that dark interior move? Mrs Peel?

MRS PEEL: If you, with all your heroic medals, say.

MACQUEEN: A sort of *shimmer*, madam.

MRS PEEL: (flirtatious) You say so, do you?

MCQUEEN: (can't help whispered lewdness) How's your dark interior, madam?

MRS PEEL: (shimmeringly) Nicely closed up, thankee. Must be the weather.

MRS AYRTON: (cautionary) Daughter.

MRS PEEL: Mother?

MRS AYRTON: (a real natter) I saw nothing. I see nothing. What is the point if I am never asked? That is the thing some of us should be asking. Do you think this…'
> *(at PEEL)*
murderer would bother to ask?

PEEL: (offhandedly) Is that hole too big for you to shut?

MRS AYRTON: (now that she's got started) Who's going to

witness what this *murderer* tried to do with me in the boat yesterday?

(Nobody is volunteering. Back at PEEL)

MRS AYRTON: You!

PEEL: Isn't it bad enough I got sucked into that big hole by marrying your daughter?

MRS AYRTON: One ball, one ball!

PEEL: (rising to the cricket challenge) Do your worst, lady!

(He takes up guard on the popping crease on the piano. She has pulled a ball from out of her bodice and thunders in to bowl. He swings and misses and is clean bowled.)

PEEL: No-ball! I told the parliamentary committee no balls wouldn't be tolerated. So that's not tolerated.

MACQUEEN: Putting one's shoulder in it, an' all that.

PEEL: Quite, but the MCC didn't envisage a shoulder like that.

MACQUEEN: (lewdly to MRS PEEL) Quite right too. Keep the hemlines well out of gumming things up, eh?

(She giggles, much to everyone's growing disgust)

PEEL: Lieutenant Macqueen, don't try claiming you are a product of the Royal Regiment; just behave yourself, sir.

MRS AYRTON: (not to be denied) This man here can deny

it all he wants, but I had his foot in my mouth fathoms down n' sinking! He did and I was! He said say hello to Davey Jones Lock-up for me! It's Locker, you Peel you! Murderer! *Ogler*! He was endeavouring to look up my floating skirts and trying to blame his rotten foot for it!

PEEL: I was only lookin' as to why there was a spot in the Southern Ocean the sharks wouldn't go.

MRS AYRTON: Murderer! Pervert! *Ogler*!

PEEL: (really hurt) By God, *ogler*!

> *(PEEL looks over at MOCK. MOCK looks back at PEEL. They nod. They tackle her from either side.*
>
> *She makes a brave struggle but they get the gag and the behind-the-back wrist ties back on. But she refuses to 'go down'; she struggles away and off like a beheaded chicken.*
>
> *She leaves a pause behind, which HALL begins to fill by scratching. The others start to take it up again too, and soon they are all going madly at it.)*

PEEL: (scratching the most) NO SCRATCHING!

> *(They all manage to almost stop, fingers itching)*

HALL: Dora dear, I didn't know there'd be flies with teeth.

DORA: I'm sure it's just they haven't been taught otherwise, Mr Hall.

HALL: Maybe that's it.
  (sillily impertinent)

Tickles your fancy, eh?

PEEL: (the father) Hey!

HALL: Sorry.

> *(PEEL diverts this by standing explorer-style in the*
> *centre of the piano top. He gestures 'onward', out into*
> *the interior beyond the seen edges of light:)*

PEEL: Courage, not forgetting the medicinal zinc! Courage!
Today we *colonise*!

> *(He gets a little burst of activity from the others, but*
> *that's about all)*

MACQUEEN: Perhaps tomorrow, Mr Peel.

PEEL: Today, while I feel the flow coming back! You hear
the steps of the old pavilion creaking and you know it's your
turn at bat!
> *(and)*
You first and I'll follow… just finishing padding up,
metaphorically speaking if metaphorical speaking is known
down here. Yes, tomorrow. Maybe you're right.

MOCK: Tomorrer. 'Ere, why?

PEEL: Mock my man, I need time to consider why I
shouldn't wait until tomorrow and simply know from
experience that by then tomorrow will have come before you
even know it. And if, you see, tomorrow comes before you
even know it, it's far better to sit here today and prepare for it
before it… can do that. It's all in the orderly. And didn't I tell
the parliamentary committee that if there wasn't an orderly
decision there wouldn't be any tomorrows? I did, sir! These

are the sort of orderly things that occupy minds today for things tomorrow. Or jolly well ought to be.

MACQUEEN: About that-there us going before, Mr Peel…
        (refers to camp along beach)
The people say they ain't quite up to it an' prefer following. Still drying out a few last crinolines, I believe. Still wringing out their hearts being dashed on the rocks, they say.
        (the dasher to MRS PEEL)
But none so fine a crinoline as some I knows, madam. Please don't take it personally.

MRS PEEL: I am certainly not taking it as personally as those…
        (re common people down beach)
workers were dragging me up the beach.

MACQUEEN: Did you manage to hang onto it, madam?

MRS PEEL: I did. I said, cads, 'ands off! I've been hanging onto it all me livelong! I told 'em, right to their nondescripts! Especially if one's paid for it far more than they could afford.

MACQUEEN: My purse awaits emptying, Mrs Peel! It's in the sac of things!

        *(She giggles coquettishly yet again, even enough to
        annoy PEEL himself, waves dismissively in direction of
        the along-the-beach camp)*

PEEL: Pikers! Most of them started wilting after nothing more than fifty days up on deck.
        (sudden thought)
What silly bugger was actually up on deck to count that off anyway?
        (no one admits knowing)

20

Make a note: next time don't forget the shade cloth. Or no recruiting any baldies, first to go down. One or the other. I prefer the shade cloth option. Or bring hats next time.
(then)
The thing is: did I get them here safely or did I not? So we had a slight accident arriving on the brine. Different salts to the brine here, you know, makes a ship a bit more rocky on the rocks. Besides, what's a bit of water on the brine, anyway, ha ha!

MACQUEEN: They dry out and they'll be ready'n'eager to go, let us not worry about that!

PEEL: (eye-glassing along beach) God sakes, little wonder they've got all those rashes there. Huddled together like drowned... I won't say it, because I frankly have never seen a cackle of drowned rats with rashes. Not huddled, I haven't.
(swings on to assembly)
Anyone?

HALL: With rashes, sir?

PEEL: That's what I said.
(no one puts hand up)
Mock, where does the word 'huddle' come from?

MOCK: Sure I dunno, mighty sir.

PEEL: Yes, you do.

MOCK: No, I don't.

PEEL: You said you did.

MOCK: No, I didn't, mighty sir.

21

PEEL: I distinctly remember you did.

MOCK: Not me, mighty sir.

PEEL: Do you have to be so contrary all the time, fellow?

MOCK: It'd help if me outfit didn't huddle, mighty sir.

PEEL: Clothes don't huddle, Mock.

MOCK: They do around the crutch if they're huddling there due to sea-water shrinkage, mighty sir.

PEEL: Clothes do not huddle, Mock, even under drowning conditions.

MOCK: Mine do. It'd help if I had another set.

PEEL: Frugalcy.

MOCK: Beg yours?

PEEL: Frugalcy.

MOCK: 'Ere, just take a moment t'jot that down, mighty sir…

> *(and while MOCK licks the top of his pencil stub, and finds FRED PEEL's back to rest his piece of paper against, while PEEL becomes kindly schoolteacher:)*

PEEL: Frugalcy, Mock.

MOCK: I knows how to spell it, mighty sir, just doan't know what it means.

PEEL: (interested) How do you spell it?

(MOCK shows him piece of paper. PEEL looks quizzically at him, gets affirmative nod of spelling. PEEL shakes his head 'well-what-do-you-know?')

PEEL: The thing is, Mock, one outfit 'nough. You're back here in your native thingmabob, after all, I might conceivably be able to find a new livery for you, but where the deuce would I ever be able to find moth holes for it? Do you even have moths down here? Any the way, by all parliamentary-committee reports that concerned me, you should be shedding your clothes by now, not putting in claims for covering what you should be ashamed of up. If you were truly going about going native again, which you jolly well should be, you have no rights to be ashamed of it. That's not *native*, man!

MOCK: No, mighty sir.

PEEL: By gaddery, we should be seeing how God made you antipodeans by now. For our people down there, it would be good on-the-job training, don'tee know, hmm? Does your tribe… or any of the tribes here… have a few spare mothballs, if you said you have moths?

MOCK: For that, like, we used to have what some beetles'd be rolling around, mighty sir, but I don't know about these days. Beetles are notorious in changin' their minds.

PEEL: Mock?
   (gets attention)
Do you expect anyone to believe that?
   (gets a surly shrug)
Don't talk nonsense, man. Beetles rolling things around. I distinctly told the parliamentary committee I wouldn't be taking any nonsense and that is nonsense. Now, are you going

23

to show us what you look like naturally or not?

MOCK: No, mighty sir.

PEEL: I bet if I was Sir Joseph Banks you wouldn't be shaking your head.

MOCK: Oh, I'd show him. He's seen it all anyways.

PEEL: Which reminds me… has anyone seen hide nor hide of any of the other native chappies? Hairy'd or just hurrying by? They have to be here somewhere.

FRED PEEL: (can't stop himself) With or without the moth holes, Father?

PEEL: (disgustedly at wife) Madam, if you can't put that person back in the bottle, kindly put him back in the womb.

> *(As a blind side play which PEEL misses, she pats her stomach and mouths the words 'the bottle' lewdly to MACQUEEN, who enjoys it immensely.*
>
> *But by now they have all turned glum, and starting to itch collectively again)*

PEEL: (as if by continuation) Frugalcy.

MOCK: (affirming) Frugalcy.

PEEL: Didn't I tell you, Mock old chap.

MOCK: You did, mighty sir.
    (and, encouraged)
Like I said, it's real frugalcy about them huddlin' of them clothes, mighty sir.

PEEL: I said, clothes don't huddle, Mock. You really oughtn't go around telling your fellow natives that our clothes huddle, you know. How are we going to get them into them?

MOCK: (shrugs) Me?, I'm only a humble Abo of the huddled class, ain't it?

PEEL: Well, well, you are forgiven even before I know you're going to deliberately forget to apologise.

MOCK: No, I wasn't, mighty sir.

PEEL: Yes, oo was.

MOCK: Ere, that'd be the day.

PEEL: Don't argue!

MOCK: 'Ere, where does 'frugalcy' come from, if I can't argue?

PEEL: Are you arguing the toss, fellow?

MOCK: Who me, mighty sir?

MACQUEEN: (the interceder) Mock old man, the toss's been tossed. We Englishman; we noble, you savage. You should never, ever, forget your apologies. Do you like your English breakfasts, Mock?

MOCK: Not 'alf.

MACQUEEN: Apologies are just like porridges, Mock, my man.

MOCK: Never thought of it that way.

MACQUEEN: (aside to MRS PEEL) They try hard.

(MOCK starts dusting off a bit of the piano top knowing that reverting to domestic duties will make him ignored again.

PEEL is again looking down to the people's camp down the beach through his eye glass)

PEEL: I supposed being huddled together rather rattily means they'll get to know each other better. Brings the rashes closer together, what?, ha ha.

MACQUEEN: They're down to their last blankets, Mr Peel. Requisition chitties are being a bit blocked, I'm afraid.

PEEL: Who's blocking them?

MACQUEEN: The tide, I think.

PEEL: Place the box above the high-tide mark, shall we? That satisfy them?

MACQUEEN: You know, it damn well could.

PEEL: Well, break out the stores, man! Where is the stores, by the way?

MOCK: (going pen and paper) 'Ere, is that 'is' or 'are'?

MACQUEEN: (ignoring him) Pretty much right here under your thumb, Mr Peel.

PEEL: Don't break out the stores! What's a bit of *huddling* but showing an honest-to-goodness solidarity? By the way, where is that chaplain?

FRED PEEL: He went under, Father.

PEEL: Did anyone managed to find out where he kept that cross for the church?

HALL: It's said it went down with him, Mr Peel.

PEEL: Blast! A bit on the selfish side, that. As if he was the only one in troubled waters.

MRS PEEL: Thomas!

PEEL: (rebuked) Well, he was Baptist and supposed to know how to dog paddle, woman. How many *did* survive anyway, has anyone asked?

MACQUEEN: The chaplain seems to be one of the few unlucky ones.

PEEL: Typical Baptist, making off with good inventory. The only thing they picked up from Rome. Well, then, certainly don't break out the stores. Who in their right mind would think we brought enough to go around, anyway?

MACQUEEN: Well, you know how the average fellow gets all high-blown, like, Mr Peel.

PEEL: I do. By rights, you have to keep an armed guard on the practise pitch.
    (then, rally-to-arms)
But, enough of these pleasantries! Get 'em going, Lieutenant! Get 'em out there settling or something! Let me know when the path's made for the piano and we'll give it a good go, eh?

Did I say tomorrow? Looking at them down there, tomorrow might be jumping things a bit.

MACQUEEN: Mind you, there's the two or more… difficult to keep count really… in sick bay from trying to get your personals ashore, Mr Peel.

PEEL: Where's the sick bay?

MACQUEEN: About where the chitty box is, Mr Peel.

PEEL: ('I have to think of everything?') Well, get it above the tide line too!

MACQUEEN: Proving a bit difficult apparently.

PEEL: Why?

MACQUEEN: It's stuck in the sand.

PEEL: Dig it out!

MACQUEEN: Seems once something's dug in down here, it stays in. An' who would've thought things like real waves?

PEEL: Godsbold, get rid of all that huddling an' get something done! I told the parliamentary committee there'd be no slack bums! And that definitely included numb bums! I'm getting exhausted here just thinking about it.

HALL: (loud in helpful) It's all the things to think about, Mr Peel.

PEEL: I know, I know.

(He turns, returns to centre of piano and stares for a
28

long time back up at 'his' sun. Finally, he turns back to their waiting on him:)

PEEL: Did we ever get that foreman back from falling overboard?

MACQUEEN: No, sir. He said he'd rather try swimming.

HALL: (piping up) The first few cases of hernias known in the colony, Mr Peel! In the sick bay. Getting your personals ashore, sir, as the lieutenant here says.

PEEL: Damn'n'dash it, Lt Macqueen, halfway decent, an' one's supposed to get hernias from a piano if you're mad enough to stay on it when it's riding a wave to shore.
   (disgusted)
Sick bay.

HALL: But what I mean to say, sir, is…
   (the sycophant)
your piano is the first piano to give a hernia in the colony, Mr Peel!

   (He gets a proud peck on the cheek from DORA PEEL)

PEEL: Precisely, and quite right too. That should go in the records.
   (back 'at' main camp down beach)
Damn'n'blast 'em, I'm trying to start a new world here!
   (then)
By the way, Lieutenant, where will we put the shining lights?

MACQUEEN: Up on the hill, Mr Peel!

PEEL: That's the ticket.
   (stops)

29

You found a hill?

MACQUEEN: We will never rest until we do, old man!

PEEL: That mean you still haven't given up about tracking down a tree?

MACQUEEN: Daily patrols sent out, Mr Peel!

(PEEL scans the horizon looking for a tree or hill. He is looking out to sea, though)

FRED PEEL: Trees and hills are probably the other way, Father.

PEEL: (at MRS PEEL) Madam, keep that creature of yours in his place.

MRS PEEL: I will not.

MACQUEEN: (finally) We could sort of build one.

PEEL: A hill, you mean?
    (to the other's nod)
Absolutely. Or, hopefully, Mock here will ask his fellow blackies if they've come across one.

MOCK: What?

PEEL: Blackies, Mock. Darkies.

MOCK: 'Ere, you spend half your day out in this sun with no hat and see how *you* look.

(PEEL goes to argue with him again, but stops on reflection:)

30

PEEL: My man Mock is right. Who said 'tomorrow'?

MOCK: You did, mighty sir.

PEEL: I did not.

MOCK: You did.

PEEL: Damn it, fellow, why would I be asking if I'd said it?

MOCK: Beats me, mighty sir.

PEEL: Just write that down and remember it.

MOCK: What's that?

PEEL: That you should at least remember what you ought to be jotting down.

MOCK: (conceding that) Fair 'nough.

PEEL: Whoever did say 'tomorrow', I want to know why. What 'tomorrow'?
    (angrily up at 'his' unflinching sun again)
Somebody tell me what tomorrow when this thing doesn't move! *And why it doesn't move?*

> *(But as much as he stands his ground to stare it down, 'his' sun doesn't oblige him. He is so outraged, he swings around to… of course… take it out on FRED PEEL)*

PEEL: You!

FRED PEEL: Father?

PEEL: (further enflamed) See, that. *That*. 'Father'! Like there's no tomorrow!
(and)
Right, you, listen up: 'Father' says hawk.

(Poor FRED searches the sky, can't see one.)

FRED PEEL: Father…?

PEEL: (coughing, spitting gestures) Hawk, you silly bugger.

(Understanding now, the son hawks up and spits theatrically)

PEEL: I said *say* 'hawk'.

FRED PEEL: Hawk.

PEEL: Again.

(His son clears his throat, spits up again)

FRED PEEL: Hawk.

(Perversely, driven on – through imperious gesturing – FRED PEEL coughs up and repeats 'hawk' a half dozen times, until PEEL gets tired of the game…)

PEEL: Yeah, yeah.

MOCK: (breaching the silence) Mighty sir, what next, now you say?

PEEL: Me? I'm going on a tour of inspection, that's what I'm going to do, Mock, old fellow.

(While the others make room for him, PEEL strides out to circumnavigate the piano three times, 'inspecting' as he goes, and:)

PEEL: Weighty affairs, Mock. Not to be hawked upon upon an open sky that
(up at 'his' unerring sun)
some sloppy sod should have shut the door on before enticing us to come here, frankly. Weighty, weighty affairs. Weighty enough to be kept damn spanking clean, let me tell you. As in unblinking. Leave it to us, above your station, hmmm? Blinking not coming naturally. Not proper blinking, that is.
(finishes 'inspection')
All very unsatisfactory.
(and)
Where is that elusive Lieutenant MacQueen?

MACQUEEN: (right next to him) Here.

PEEL: If you were from the Navy, Macqueen, you'd seen there's a lot more make-and-mend to be done before I can give over a 'satisfactory'.

MACQUEEN: (quite openly) What say you, Mrs Peel?

MRS PEEL: Oh, I would certainly give over a 'satisfactory'.

MACQUEEN: (lewd) Nothing more?

MRS PEEL: (ditto) Well, we could always see what's one up from satisfactory.

PEEL: (disgusted, but knowingly) Mrs Peel, your slurp is showing.

MACQUEEN: Slurp, slurp!

> *(She cackles openly, and PEEL has to click his tongue with annoyance; obviously has to take head-of-the-family stock)*

.

PEEL: Wife, dragon ma-in-law, daughter…
> *(at FRED PEEL)*

runt…
> *(at MACQUEEN and HALL)*

suckholes, and…
> *(at MOCK)*

home-grown an' still trying, so seven out of ten…
> *(stops forgetfully; to MOCK)*

What was I about to say?

MOCK: Something mighty.

PEEL: I don't think so.

MOCK: I do.

PEEL: No, you do not.

MOCK: Yes, I do.
> *(turns to others)*

Discussing things with th'master here, always learns me how to express what I thinks.

PEEL: *Teaches* me how to express what I *think*.

MOCK: (to all) See what I mean?

> *(Due to MACQUEEN's close attention, MRS PEEL finds herself game enough to tackle PEEL openly, points especially to her trussed-up mother:)*

MRS PEEL: (accusing) You said bring mummy.

PEEL: I didn't say alive.

MRS PEEL: You said it'd be cheaper on a family rate.

PEEL: I didn't know she'd need crating up. Expensive, that crating.

MRS PEEL: That was a pork barrel with scrapings, sir!

PEEL: If it was pork, I had to pay for it to be thrown overboard.

MRS PEEL: It was rotten!

PEEL: It wasn't until she stuck her nose into it.

MRS PEEL: My mummy's tied up!

PEEL: She can go and get knotted!

MRS PEEL: (to FRED) Freddie, unhemp Granny's hump.

(FRED goes to do so, but stops dead at MRS AYRTON to:)

FRED PEEL: Are we sure we want to scare off anything within shooting distance, Mother? Ha ha, father.

(Annoyed, she pushes him aside and unties and ungags her mother herself.

As soon as she is free, MRS AYRTON launches into her blue-murder routine again:)

MRS AYRTON: HELP! MURDER! RAPE! OGLING HERE!

> *(Even MRS PEEL joins in to re-gag and re-tie her again)*

MRS PEEL: (outcry) Thomas, this has gone too far!

PEEL: Not a step further, my dear, I promise.

MRS PEEL: I want to go home!

PEEL: (too much to hope for:) Will you take your mother?

MRS PEEL: No! Yes!

PEEL: I'll throw in a proper crate this time.

> *(She half-swoons with grave indecision. Of course, MACQUEEN is there to catch her. Mindless, anyway, PEEL begins another tour around the piano)*

PEEL: Mock, keep up!

> *(MOCK quickly falls into step with his employer. They complete three turns about... PEEL kicking FRED PEEL out of the way each time... while PEEL throws quizzical looks back at 'his' unerring sun again and:)*

PEEL: Interesting. Interesting.

MOCK: What be that, mighty sir?

PEEL: (re sun) I've spoken to it. I've asked about it. I've even spoken *about* it, but it will not move. That is my opinion about it, anyway, Mock, and if you'd keep up, you might see why.

MOCK: Why, mighty sir?

PEEL: Because that-there sun thing is unsettling for to start a settlement under, Mock, and why else you ask?

MOCK: I dunno settlement things, mighty sir, only about what's taken away, like.

PEEL: Everything thing is not about you, Mock.

MOCK: (genuinely) Isn't it?

PEEL: No, it is not.

MOCK: That's a pity, mighty sir.

PEEL: (stopping) Yes, it is rather.
    (then swings around to MACQUEEN)
Well, get on with it, man!

MACQUEEN: I'll bite.

PEEL: (waving hand generally) Move them out in some order and in some general direction! Not seawards or up or down, that is. You know what I mean.

MACQUEEN: I thought you said tomorrow?

PEEL: (imperial) If you leave it until tomorrow I would have told the parliamentary committee we would tomorrow's borrowers be, man. And never a tomorrow's borrower be!

MACQUEEN: (getting it) And how could you follow

tomorrow…?

PEEL: Exactly.
(afterthought)
And take my wife and family with you.

MACQUEEN: (re trussed-up MRS AYRTON) We don't
have the pack horses for it, Mr Peel.

PEEL: Well, well, leave her but send back something.

MACQUEEN: Like what?

PEEL: I don't know, man. This place's been here for… oh,
what?, a thousand years?… maybe even more! It must have
something lying around that could bear her up.

> *(MACQUEEN 'gathers' the others to lead them off,*
> *obviously signalling the main camp down the beach to*
> *move out into the interior as he does so)*

PEEL: (after them) If you do find something that'll bear her
up, let me know an' we'll patent it!

> *(MOCK has stayed behind and is now looking at PEEL*
> *obviously wanting to go with the others. Finally, PEEL*
> *waves him off to follow. MOCK does a quick dust-off of*
> *the piano top, rights the cricket wicket, puts the cricket*
> *bat neatly leaning against it, then eagerly follows*
> *MACQUEEN and co.*
>
> *When finally alone… albeit with MRS AYRTON… PEEL*
> *can give in to a bout of manic scratching)*

PEEL: Aaah. Ooo.
(turns his back to his mother-in-law)

Give's a scratch, atta girl…

(She tries to kick him. He has to pull away. He goes, scratchily, to take up guard with the bat, and:)

PEEL: C'mon, your best shot, old girl…!

(Never to be beaten by him, she drops to her knees, tries to pick up the ball in her teeth but, gag-bound, cannot. So she picks it up backwards – her hands tied behind her back – and tries very heroically running in to bowl backwards.

The ball only trickles out of her hand. PEEL gleefully leaps at it where it stops and after a couple of attempts manages to give it a good whack)

PEEL: Four, four!
        (and triumphantly)
Now, *that*, the parliamentary committee will get to know about when it comes in off the park. As soon as the beach head was properly established, things pathetic worthy of being struck for four were struck for four. No mercy was shown. But the new flashing blade was.

(It doesn't stop her staring daggers at him.

Blackout.)

39

ACT 2

3.

(Darkened stage. Much snoring in the middle of a night.

The unerring sun-on-Peel gradually comes up on him again. He is sitting with arms on knees staring up at it, even though there is night around him and, at its shadowed fringes people obviously sleeping.

MOCK lights a weak lamp, comes forward to PEEL.)

MOCK: Mighty sir…

PEEL: Don't try to pretend you didn't see that, Mock.

MOCK: See what?

PEEL: Now, see, you are trying to pretend when I asked you not to, fellow.

MOCK: No, I ain't, mighty sir.

PEEL: Yes, you are.

MOCK: Ain't, honestly, like.

PEEL: Are. And it ain't ain't. Aren't. And it ain't aren't. It's are. Write that down before I forget you ought.

MOCK: (not doing so) Thankee.
 (then)
What are I ain't, mighty sir?

PEEL: (up at sun) See it move.

MOCK: See what move?

PEEL: That blasted sun.

MOCK: Oh, right. Still there in the middle of the night, be it?

PEEL: It definitely moved. It could be a very good day today, Mock!

> *(MOCK puts a blanket around his shoulders, makes sure he is comforted, then goes back to his sleeping spot.*
>
> *Now only the light of 'his' unerring sun once more. And the snoring around the piano of the others)*

PEEL: Mock?

MOCK: Mighty sir?

PEEL: How long's it been?

MOCK: Nigh a month, mighty sir.

PEEL: Could be real movements all round today, Mock.

MOCK: Right you are.

PEEL: Mock?

MOCK: Here.

PEEL: Surprised you haven't scarpered, Mock.

MOCK: What for?

PEEL: Revert to type, how it goes.

MOCK: Too many tribal fellahs out there, mighty sir.

PEEL: Stop dusting yourself down, man. Show them the real you.

MOCK: Argumentative types.

PEEL: Exactly. So?

MOCK: I'm given all that up, mighty sir. Them spears hurt.

PEEL: Good night, Mock.

MOCK: Nightie night, mighty sir.

(The night 'returns' around 'his' unerring sun, as does the snoring around.

Now it is FRED PEEL's turn to come out of the shadows to tend to his father. He eases him from his seated position to lie down, gets a pillow for his head etc.

PEEL has a violent sleeping moment. His son soothes him down, and then, lamentedly:)

FRED PEEL: Expression
bursts to get out.
Expression
just bursts
and hurts.

(He is surprised when the older man speaks to him as he goes, and almost civilly:)

PEEL: How's those bites?

FRED PEEL: Not too festering, Father.

PEEL: Get something put on 'em.

FRED PEEL: It's all in your medicine bag, I think, Father.

PEEL: Hands orf!
    (then cunningly)
Spit's good they say. Didn't I tell you to hawk sometime
back?

FRED PEEL: You did, Father.

PEEL: Well, then, you know what to do with it, don't you?

FRED PEEL: What might that be, Father?

PEEL: The spit, the spit!

FRED PEEL: Thank you, Father.

PEEL: Don't thank me. You're the one come out of your
mother's body. No wonder the blasted flies won't leave you
alone.

FRED PEEL: My lot I expect, Father.

    ('His' unerring sun fades, as all does to the snoring.)

4.

*(Snoring resumes. 'His' unerring sun resumes. PEEL
is sleeping like a baby, well after daybreak.*

A barge pole comes and prods him dozily awake. It is held by MRS AYRTON)

MRS AYRTON: Up n' at 'em. That'd be the day.

PEEL: Where's Mock?
    (she shrugs)
What was he doing just here?
    (she shrugs)
Where that bastard?

MRS AYRTON: Might you mean that rightful son my daughter had to go through sex to give you? Well…

> *(She shrugs again, then ignores him to proceed with chores. He squints up at 'his' unerring sun)*

MRS AYRTON: You should do something about that snoring while you sit around here snoring. It's bad enough them searching for hills'n'trees without trying to find out where all the birds've gone.

PEEL: (shaking head) Nope, no snoring.

MRS AYRTON: Ha. My daughter says she can't even hear herself snoring. That's saying something right there.

PEEL: It's *snorting*. Few can. It comes with the lineage, doan'tee know. Where's breakfast?

MRS AYRTON: ('who cares?') It's still on the hoof, that snorting.

> *(He leaps up with an alarming burst of energy, grabs bat, takes guard)*

PEEL: I'm sick of you! Let's have your worst! Today I'm the crashing-into-the-ropes king!

MRS AYRTON (now snorts) You ain't even laid bat on ball yet.

PEEL: Oh yeah? What about that four that time?

MRS AYRTON: You must have been dreaming. Like going on about Mock -- or about our little Freddie's being here. What's wrong with you?

PEEL: (sudden downcast) Must have been why I felt queer trying to speak nice to him. Son? What a bastard!
    (then)
Still no Mock?

MRS AYRTON: Off beatin' around the bush.

PEEL: What's 'beatin' around the bush', woman? Who wants to take bush, start going around beating it? Speak sense or not at all.

(She evidently points the other camp down the beach)

MRS AYRTON: That's what them down there are calling it.

PEEL: (deigning to look) Seems to be more of them.

MRS AYRTON: (nodding) Word was there was a ship coming in leaving for home. They're gathering back here just in case it's true.

PEEL: (calls out) Deserters!

(gets indistinguishable insults shouted back. He quickly turns back to stare at 'his' unerring sun – and, finally, with sadness:)

PEEL: I dreamt I saw it move.

MRS AYRTON: You on about that whatever again? No wonder my little Dorie says that through the occasional telescope's near enough to you.

PEEL: That's calumny!

MRS AYRTON: Might be, if there's such a word.

PEEL: See, you don't even know what you're talking about. That's my daughter you're talking calumniously about.

MRS AYRTON: There you go again, stuck up. Always when Mock's book ain't around to find out what you mean. You murderer. *Looker.*

PEEL: (waving it off) Are we all sure it's been more than a month?

MRS AYRTON: Who's 'all'?
    (then, a moment to get wound up)
Murderer! Pervert! Looker! You're ruining my family I had!

> *(It bucks PEEL up to hear it. He jumps to his feet, plays childish chords on the piano – barely making piano sounds now – to orchestrate her chorusing:)*

MRS AYRTON: Murderer! Dirty pervert! Looker! I've seen you!

> *(But this does nothing but rejuvenate him. He grabs bat,*

46

renews guard, challenges her to bowl to him, but she shows contempt. Anyway, he has to stop for:)

PEEL: Where's the ball?
(she doesn't deign to respond)
Fuck, did you eat it again? Did you open your mouth and it got sucked up? Woman, do you realise, if we call here Western Australia, it won't be because of the abundance of cricket balls? Are you even bothering to keep *count*?

MRS AYRTON: What do you care?

PEEL: I was England's most famous 12th man! Why, out of all England, is it you who needs the reminding?

MRS AYRTON: You ain't even ever raised any bat other than that one there, and where your mind goes, it don't.

PEEL: (high horse) If that were possibly so, it would only be because there was always someone ready'n'eager to carry it for me.

MRS AYRTON: 12th man! You ain't ever made a run.

PEEL: Because I was back keeping the pavilion I built and paid for fit for lunch and tea. Trays. Real buggers to keep up, trays. And *very* famously too, if you take other 12th men! No comparison. Miss it already.

MRS AYRTON: Stupid game anyway.

PEEL: This game, madam… which you are experiencing beginner's luck at… goes way, way back. My own grandfather codified the rule he could be in the team and didn't have to bat. Peel tradition, that. Out in the middle, when we Peels nod, it does not mean prima facie that the bowler may commence, but that the bat should be picked up and handed over.

MRS AYRTON: Back to Henry the 8th's time now, are we?

PEEL: ('yep') Drop a catch, lose your noggin.

MRS AYRTON: Before the Vikings, I spose?

PEEL: Every year, they sent their best 11 with armies of fans. Talk about ham fisted. Got sent packing.

MRS AYRTON: Before Jesus's time?

PEEL: First recorded nomination of a 13th man. Had to cover for Judas.
     (and)
Goes to show it goes back before your time, even.

MRS AYRTON: (prissily) I'd like my gag and ropes put back on now, thank you.

PEEL: (stubborn no) Too easy.

MRS AYRTON: Then I have a suggestion. Why don't you just take up your bat and ball and go home. I'll go with you.
     (cheers from down the beach)
Them too.

PEEL: And I might just do that. Could do with a bit of shade.

MRS AYRTON: (sees opening) My little lovey Dorie says her lot's got all the shade you'd need...
     (points off into 'dark' interior)
in there.

PEEL: (scandalised) That's not shade! In there…
   (shudders)
that's *shelter*. That's giving up on real shade for shelter from
a bit of wattle and a bit of daub, especially when they can't
even find the wattle and don't know what daub is! A Peel
does not give up real shade that's stood the test of time! A
Peel refuses shelter when it is handed out as charity!
   (craftily)
But you go and take shelter.

MRS AYRTON: I ain't leaving you alone to…
   (shouts)
'Murderer!, pervert!' any other poor innocent.
   (then to his resulting surliness)
'Ere, string up a bit of shade cloth here.

PEEL: (fatally) Wouldn't I like to.

MRS AYRTON: (encouraging) I'd be in that.

PEEL: (painfully) It wouldn't be proper shade. It's be
manufacturing shade out of nothing. Shade should come at a
price.

MRS AYRTON: G'arn, it would. I'd help you.

PEEL: How could that make it proper shade? My old father
used to say: 'Do not erect shade from droopy drawers'.

MRS AYRTON: (no idea of what meant) That so?

PEEL: (up at 'his' sun) That bloody thing shouldn't be there!
You can't put up shade for something that shouldn't be there,
anyone knows that. That's shouldn't-be-there shade, that is.
It's basic mathematics about planets and stars n' things.

49

MRS AYRTON: (really confused) What shouldn't be there?

PEEL: I've already told the parliamentary committee enough of the shady, snidey 'I-shouldn't-be there's. I *am* here, and I ain't moving. Parliamentary committee or no parliamentary committee.

MRS AYRTON: You should move into a bit of shade.

PEEL: Sadly, I have just explained that I am a Peel.

MRS AYRTON: You're peeling all over, that's what you are.

(He returns to sulky aloneness, goes back to sitting on piano top, staring back at 'his' sun, arms on knees, mumbling.

MRS AYRTON stands looking contemplatively at him before she turns and calls down to the other camp down the beach, holding out her bound wrists for attention:)

MRS AYRTON: Oi, you lot. I can handle the gag m'self; anyone deft with ropes? A butcher among you, deft at putting a gal out of her misery?

(Blackout)

5.
(First, PEEL's sun, and then general early-morning lighting.

They have all returned once more and are back to be positioned around the piano.

PEEL, preoccupied by 'his' yet-unerring sun on him, is unmindful of their presence. None of their clearing throats or loud relief from scratching madly at the sand fly bites distract him.

Finally, PEEL calls:)

PEEL: Lieutenant Macqueen!

MACQUEEN: (coming onto the piano) Here.

(PEEL stares down at the other's feet, until MACQUEEN removes himself from the piano. PEEL meets him metaphorically half-way by leaning over and holding out -- up to the sun -- a V with his fingers... motions MACQUEEN to take a bead on the sun through it. MACQUEEN's great reluctance to indulge PEEL is countered by MRS PEEL silently urging him to pacify PEEL)

PEEL: What do you see there, man?

MACQUEEN: (not seeing anything) Sky?

PEEL: Any clouds?

MACQUEEN: No clouds.

PEEL: Keep looking. Don't blink.
    (then)
You blinked.

MACQUEEN: I was preparing for not blinking.

PEEL: No excuses, man, just tell me what you see.

MACQUEEN: Blue s…

PEEL: Wait for it, wait for it!
  (starts measured counting up to 10)
One, two, three… etc
  (then, after)
Well?

MACQUEEN: Well, what?

PEEL: Did it move, man? I thought it moved!

MACQUEEN: What moved, where?

PEEL: (pointing at sun) Don't be mad. All I am trying to
ascertain from you is do you or do you not think that-there sun
has moved more than, say, a few weeks' worth?

MACQUEEN: (indulging) Oh absolutely!

PEEL: (hopefully) More than a month?

MACQUEEN: Oh absolutely too!

PEEL: How much more?

MACQUEEN: (for help) Mr Hall?

HALL: ('leaving' DORA to:) Absolutely.

PEEL: A month or more, eh?

MACQUEEN and HALL: Absolutely!

PEEL: Who'da thought.
  (and then just noticing them all:)

For God's sake, why do I have to look around and find you all back here for?

MRS PEEL: (towards the bound-and-gagged her) Are you looking after my mother, Thomas?

PEEL: Hand on bible?

MRS PEEL: That's what I want.

PEEL: Sorry, the bible went down with the chaplain.
    (waving towards 'dark' interior)
Now, get going! I ain't 'nursie'.

DORA: We're just trying to gather our breath, Father.

PEEL: Don't you 'Father' me like that unless you're so far away you need a foghorn! I've got to report progress. *Progress.* You lot are not making *progress.* You need to venture out of the crease. Kindly tell me who doesn't know that?

    (He gets no riposte)

MACQUEEN: We thought we might try a little trying-again, old son. Try it from scratch, see how we go. Didn't we, Hall?

HALL: (prodded by DORA) I think so.

PEEL: (the stern leader) You are definitely not going to start all over again. Starting all over again is a willful waste of stores, and I won't have it. Sitting back here watching stores is no fun you know, but someone has to have a hand in it.

MRS PEEL: (brave representative) Well, Thomas, we did get up the shade… which was very nice for our Louis the Two

Double Brass Canopy Half-Tester marital bed…

PEEL: Our what?

MRS PEEL: Our Louis the Two Double Brass Canopy Half-Tester marital bed.

PEEL: You didn't bring that along, did you?

MRS PEEL: I liked the way it bounces, you know that.
    (smutty looks pass between her and MACQUEEN)
I didn't know nice until I tried it in a new position. Do you know back home it bounced up'n'down and here it bounces down'n'up?

PEEL: No, I don't know. Get on with it.

MRS PEEL: (not to be hurried) You should know, Thomas, that that Louis the Two Double Brass Canopy Half-Tester marital bed of ours has never been more comfortable on the down'n'up, even the up'n'down. It being where it is now. At first, it was only good really for holding on while they carried it hinter-wise. But after that absolute blighter of a flood and they cornered the shade and tied it down, well… as a bed, it has certainly got its marital back, which is what I am saying.

PEEL: What is this woman talking about? Shade, drought? No shade, no drought!

MRS PEEL: … And then, you see, the rains came and flooded us right out.

PEEL: No flood, no rain!

MRS PEEL: Do you know that our Louis the Two Double Brass Canopy Half-Tester marital bed floats? Did you ever test it, Thomas, before it was embarked on half way around the world? It floated right away, you know. Slip, slip, slop slop. It went right down that river there like a swan. So they called it the Swan. The river and the bed actually. I don't know after which one they're calling it black though.

MACQUEEN: (a coo) Should be able to find it somewhere, Mrs Peel, while we're choofing looks around for any hill or trees.

PEEL: And that other thing.

MACQUEEN: What other thing's that?

PEEL: Can't remember. Something important… gone missing.

MACQUEEN: (carries on) Natives won't know what to do with oak in that-there bed, ma'am. No oak here. I think. Hall?...

HALL: I don't think so.

PEEL: (at him) No oak? No English backbone?
      (HALL shakes his head sadly)
No stumps, no bails?
      (HALL shakes his head a little more sadly)
Willow?
      (HALL shakes his head very much more sadly)
No bats?

      (HALL has to shrug 'what can I say'. PEEL is so angry, he turns back to stare at 'his' sun, but soon his anger make him revert back to the conversation)

PEEL: No rain, no floating!

(He jumps off the piano in a pique, runs around quite madly pointing up at the unerring sun, trying to get them to see the sheer logic of:)

PEEL: No shade, no rains, no floating! Look! Look! Macqueen, Macqueen…
   (grabs him by the arm, shove him towards sun)
did you see it move more than a minute, man?
   (to MACQUEEN's dumbness)
All right, two minutes?!
   (ditto)
All right, five. Maximum five!

(Releases the lieutenant, stands confused by himself. Crestfallen he returns to the piano top, practises taking guard at the popping crease line but even this is desultory.

Finally, MRS AYRTON removes her own hog-ties and, showing her growing influence, strides over to him… openly climbing on the otherwise sacrosanct piano-top area… removes the bat from his hand and shakes him unceremoniously into a little more calmness.

His arm goes out to hold the calf of her leg. She pushes it away but noticeably not too brusquely.

Blackout)

6.
(A new day dawning around PEEL seated rooted staring up at 'his' sun. He could have been like that all night.

The inner company – they are all there, except for MOCK -- around the piano comes to life, with more snoring giving way to more scratchings.

Finally, PEEL comes to life and, yet again, angrily:)

PEEL: I don't care what anyone says…
  (up at 'his' sun)
I'm not moving an inch until that bloody bugger of a thing moves more than a second. One second.
  (waits in outrage)
You'd think a man was asking for anything more than a simple bloody blink.
  (up at it)
Blink, blink!
  (and)
What a stubborn place this god-forsaken place is! You come here and you pull the smallest expectation out of your kit bag, and what do you get?

(He has a good think about it, while knowing the others are finally getting all their attention upon him, then:)

PEEL: Even if any of you lot were really real, you'd still be unperfect puffs.

(They look at him blankly)

PEEL: (snapping fingers at them) Puff. Puff.

(Then swings back angrily at 'his' sun, cries out)

PEEL: Move! MOO-OOVE!

(The others might be stunned, but MOCK isn't. He is returning at this moment, looking distinctly dishevelled,

and with a new attitude of open flippancy:)

MOCK: Anyone callin' for a bit o' moo-mooooo milkin'?

(and doesn't wait for answer but simply goes to his place to put his head down, muttering before 'crashing out':)

MOCK: Be with you in a jiff, mighty sir…

(They all watch him but are obviously not going to get any more out of him. It has anyway given PEEL time to recover himself. With far more steadiness, he starts counting 'his' sun off, while the other simply watch on and scratch…)

PEEL: One, two, three, four…. ten, eleven, twelve…

(He waits a little time for it to respond but does so without expectation. He then comes back to the real situation, calls as the commander of all again, as though it was the first minute of arrival on the shore:)

PEEL: Are we ready?

MRS PEEL: Thomas, I am ready. Lieutenant Macqueen is ready. Dora is ready. Mr Hall, are you ready?

HALL: I am ready, Mrs Peel!

MRS PEEL: (meaning towards DORA) Are your intentions honourable n' steady?

HALL: They are ready'n'steady, ma'am!

MRS PEEL: (to her daughter) Dorie, do you remember the

short arm jolt I taught you?

DORA: Ready to go, mama!

> *(she gives HALL a friendly short arm jolt which still*
> *takes his breath away)*

MRS PEEL: And so we are all ready, Thomas.

PEEL: You've forgotten your mother.

MRS PEEL: Excuse me, but she is yours now.

PEEL: Rhubarb!

MRS PEEL: Look at Mock. That is no fit condition, and I've
seen a lot of fit and unfit conditions in my life.
> *(meaning her mother)*
I leave you in good hands.

PEEL: You wouldn't leave me to a gorilla! Why leave me to
those hands?
> *(to her shrug)*
And who said I'm not leading you out this time?
> *(gets all-round laughs)*
All this usurping, I am saying 'bah' to.
> *(gets more all-round laughs)*
All right. Lieutenant Macqueen, lead off, and don't look back,
sir!

> *(They sort of shuffle about but don't really make a move*
> *because PEEL obviously still isn't even pretending to)*

MACQUEEN: We'd a meeting an' would like to take the
insect bite medicine with us this time, Mr Peel.

PEEL: (with his well-oiled body) Very little to go around.
    (indicating MRS AYRTON)
That woman, when she stands tall, there's a lot needed if it's
all round you're talking about for a start. Tried squeezing a
few native leaves, have we? Seen if their leaves've got grit in
their veins down here, have we?

HALL: It's not just us, Mr Peel.
    (waving hand down to main camp)
It's all your other people. They're complaining they can't get
on coz all the itchings be turning them around in circles.

PEEL: (accusatory) They only need a good old pointer of
which way to go. By God, sir, I'd show them the way!

MACQUEEN: (joining in) That's the ticket. They say they've
seen enough of your fly-bitten front, sir. They want to see a
bit of your fly-bitten back.

PEEL: By God, they'll see the back o' my fly-bitten hand!

    *(But he is stymied by another bout of having to stare up
    at 'his' sun, which stops him in its tracks as if he is
    snared by it. Finally:)*

MACQUEEN: Peel?

MRS PEEL: Thomas?

DORA: Father?

HALL: Mr Peel?

PEEL: (half reverie) Lieutenant Macqueen, see, what you do
is show a bit of leadership, is my suggestion from the first-
eleven team sheet. You stride out with longer strides. You

out stride the hoi polloi. You get right out there and rigidize your back, sir. You look to their morals and take things from there, always leading onwards.

MACQUEEN: (not without guilt) How's that? Frankly, sir, their morals are as low as their morales, an' that's saying something. It's either love bites or fly bites, that's a fact, and the regiment didn't teach me about the second, Mr Peel. Last tally I got, twenty of 'em have snuffed it already. Could do with a bit of snuff m'self. Got any, old chap?

PEEL: (low cunning) No.

MACQUEEN: Twenty of 'em. It's either them love bites or flies, or its dysentery. What do they say they're getting, Mr Hall?

HALL: Shit to tears. Pardon.

MACQUEEN: (nodding) Aye, that... right shit to tears. Issafact, regimentally-wise.

HALL: Excuse me. They say they only want what were promised, Mr Peel. Food n' land. They'd even settle on half of one an' half of the other, you're a mind to. But they want to get off this beach once n' for good all proper. They want good old dry land where they can retch up without feeling sea sick. We've been stuck here for two months, the like. That's what they're saying. Clothes stinking, too; marriages breaking up. Won't go near each other as a result.

PEEL: ('oh, come on' derision) Two months, my eye.

MRS PEEL: Two months, Thomas!

(PEEL has a momentary confusion during which he
61

stands before the unerring sun as if for an answer,
before turning back:)

PEEL: Someone has gone out of their mind! When was the last bearing taken on it?

MACQUEEN: If you're talking about the time, you don't use sextants to take the time, Mr Peel.

PEEL: I'm not saying that!

MACQUEEN: What, then, sir?

PEEL: I'm saying use a little bloody sextant when you've…
     (slowing with forgetfulness)
gone potty with the time. Or getting potty. Or…
     (runs down)

MACQUEEN: (just trying to be helpful) Sextants. We not using them for the time. On dry land we're not, last time I heard. Not at sea neither come to think of it.

PEEL: (revs up again) In the higher reaches of the parliamentary committee they do. Sextants all over the place. You look up their minutes. A lot of things… have bearing on their minutes.
     (sees sense in indicating MRS AYRTON)
Take a look at this woman. I know it's hard, but just take a look at her. Does she look two months older?
     (gets no reply, except signalling abuse from MRS A)
Can she look two months older?

HALL: (tentatively) Maybe a shave…?

     (He gets nudged into silence by DORA)

62

PEEL: But it does seem longer than yesterday, that I grant you. What we've got to watch for is a defiant defense to start the innings. Leave a lot of good length balls go pass. Set a solid foundation.

(at 'his' sun)

And a bit of cooperation from the shade department.

('His' sun seems to blink at him. Triumphantly:)

PEEL: Macqueen!

MACQUEEN: (startled) What?

(PEEL takes a bead of 'his' sun again, this time along his arm just to be sure)

PEEL: That was a definite movement. We are making progress! Go tell all the slack sods down there to get ready. Dry off the sweat first. Lift the old armpits, sprinkle a bit of powder around. Tell 'em soon, soon!

MRS PEEL: What are you going on about now?

PEEL: Open your eyes, woman!

MRS PEEL: They are open. What does that matter in this dark?

PEEL: ('dark?') Don't you go mad on a man too. Have you ever had your eyes open when it's dark? Daylight, those eyes of yours give you a bad enough time, as it is.

MRS PEEL: It's dawn, Thomas, and you said today's the day.

PEEL: (smirk) Hands up, anybody, who thinks this noonday sun looks like dawn?

(pushing his luck at mocking her)
Hands up, anybody, who knows it's still dark and can't see me
clearly. Or can't see that everybody else but her is holding
their hands up by taking my word for it.

MRS PEEL: You promised today, Thomas.

PEEL: (not moving though) I sure did. But then I'm a Peel
and still…
    (conducts for a reply, gets no response)
… *peeling*. Belfry-wise. Ha ha.

> *(They wait unimpressed, but his self-righteous logic-*
> *snigger is apparently all they are going to get. At least*
> *PEEL is facing inland away from 'his' sun. HALL tries*
> *to encourage what he takes as an encouraging sign…)*

HALL: Mr Peel, we're all behind you. Look at them down
there, with their pots'n'pans whatsnots all in marching line.
Pointed inland, aye. Eager to try again but only if you're in
the lead, aye. Them what's left. But never mind that. There's
plenty of peas growing in their pods. They'll lay down roots,
right enogh…
    (MRS PEEL and MACQUEEN snigger together)
It ain't all sleeping and dying, they told me to tell 'e. Dead or
alive, they said, they're down there, ready to *spread*, your
grace!

MACQUEEN: (caught up with optimism) Spread 'em!

MRS PEEL: (the public joker) Not here, James!

> *(and, when turning around to her son to get his expected*
> *glad-hand response, sees that:)*

MRS PEEL: (hue and cry) Aiee, my little Freddie's gone!

DORA: My little brother's gone!

HALL: My future brother-in-law is gone!

> *(MRS AYRTON struggles to speak in same vein. They wait without helping until she gets the gag removed enough to:)*

MRS AYRTON: My future in-law grandson is gone!

> *(It stops everybody, but that is all she has for the time being.*
>
> *PEEL sees diversion from himself, flings his arms into the interior)*

PEEL: Right, everybody find my darling boy!
> *(to his wife's smile at this)*
I said 'darling boy' and I meant 'darling boy'!
> *(realises what he has just said)*
Right, I am going to the dogs! Someone find him before he's gone to the dogs too and I can show how much I retract saying that!
> *(nobody moves)*
Everybody! Macqueen, Hall…! Mock!
> *(looks down at, gives up on, snoring MOCK)*

MRS PEEL: (further outcry) My Freddie's gone to the dogs!

DORA: (ditto) My bruther Fred's gone to the dogs!

HALL: Actually, they're called dingos down here, Mr Peel.

MRS PEEL: (stopping) Who would possibly call a dog a…

HALL: Dingo.

MRS PEEL: … dingo? That's silly.

HALL: Well, you can't mistake them. They look so much like what you'd call a dog, really. This was before the natives saw our dogs in order to know they shouldn't be calling them dingos.
    (then)
Or it might have been the other way round. With dogs and dingos… you know.
    (shrugs)

MRS PEEL: (continuing) My little Freddie, come back!

    (MACQUEEN and HALL hurry off to search for him. PEEL swings onto MRS PEEL)

PEEL: You find that boy's tongue and you'll find the dogs feedin'.

MRS PEEL: I will not.

PEEL: (to nobody in particular) I'll wager the word 'bastard' isn't even coming loosely out of his mouth while his tongue's being gobbled up. You try to raise 'em right. You say, 'Say bastard', and they go 'bastard', but they don't give it any air, push comes to shove. That's where the loose tongue comes in, from outside the family line.
    (swings bitterly onto MRS PEEL)
It's all your fault. All you ever know is push, not shove! I should have known the way you dragged me back up the aisle!

MRS PEEL: You don't care about my Freddie!

(She stumbles after MACQUEEN tearfully.

PEEL rounds on DORA as the next best thing:)

PEEL: Quick, follow her, you included, before little Freddie-weddies spreads the word my loins didn't have the sense to give up after you.

DORA: (but cool as a cucumber) How's the will, papa?

PEEL: (having to stop) Unchanged from you. Why?

DORA: We have it with us?

PEEL: We have it with us.

DORA: ('good enough'; shouts after them too) That man in those dingos mouths, I've never laid eyes on!
　　(and)
Papa, I really don't mind this beastly beach with all its beachly beasts. I was thinking maybe I should stay where the will is, you know. Keep my fist about it, in case of really high tides.

PEEL: I said everybody.

(Her unmoving is cancelled out by HALL returning to lift her lovingly to her feet and to guide her off. PEEL opportunistically sees to his mother-in-law:)

PEEL: You heard. All. Everybody.

MRS AYRTON: (no way moving) You'd be lucky.

PEEL: (down to main camp) HELP!

MRS AYRTON: (easily drowning him out) MURDER!

PERVERT! OGLING!

(There is no response to either of them)

MRS AYRTON: Is there a man amongst you?!

(There obviously isn't. After waiting to see if someone would come forward, they are left with:)

PEEL: Look, lady, this is no Lady's Day at Ascot. Go away. Scoot. Go home. Go surfing in six petticoats! Leave this piano!

MRS AYRTON: What could get me home, you mentally smashed to smithereens three months ago when you threw me overboard.

PEEL: That's a lie.

MRS ARYTON: You had your foot in my mouth. Three fathoms down.

PEEL: I was trying to rescue my foot.

MRS AYRTON: Surely thou pulleth my pisser.

PEEL: Surely, thou ain't got no pisser.

MRS AYRTON: That's for me to know and you never to find out.

PEEL: (real sudden interest) Which is it?

MRS AYRTON: I tell you what it isn't. It isn't yesterday.

PEEL: What 'yesterday'? Did I say anything about any

68

yesterday?

MRS AYRTON: (brushing that aside hotly) You and your yesterday, my bum!

PEEL: That's an insult to yesterday. What did yesterday ever do to you?

MRS AYRTON: (repeat) Yesterday, my bum!

PEEL: ('all right') Yesterday, yesterday!
(but turns 'up' to 'his' unerring sun and whines)
Wasn't it?
(draws blank from it)
Was it?
(whispers intimately to it)
She said I said yesterday and you said yesterday but wasn't too explicit about it.
(still blank)
You put on the pads and wait and wait. You'd think one out of eleven would drop out occasionally, no…? You say to yourself there is absolutely nothing wrong with 12th man.

(He sits in exasperation. She tidied up around him with added proprietory, self-assurance.

Finally:)

PEEL: (to nobody) This's what you get when you promote from the lower deck. A little breeding and that blasted Captain Cook would have known he should have mentioned the twenty-four- hour sun. The lower-deck bugger should have known people would be interested in that sort of thing. Transit of Venus… *cock*! You ply the trades to get all the way down here… you tell me what saps the spirit more? Couldn't take his eyes off the bread fruit, that's what his trouble was.

69

(up at 'his' sun)
Nice'n'warm when you've got no sweat left, have to admit. A little acclimatising, n' whatnot. Mull upon the tasks ahead. The thing is not to panic when you're chasing over two hundred on the board and taking out the drinks. Avoid being found short just out of your ground, is the thing. Hot enough for fried eggs. I like fried eggs after getting smitten by an out'n'out throw on a run not called. Reminds you of the Chippendale in the drawing room in the manor in the pavilion in the frogswamp back home. What the frogswamp? What shimmers? Oh, mightily shimmers are there down here. I could get used to this if the bloody flies didn't have such big fangs'n'claws. But like I've always said, if it's itchy, scratch the bugger of a thing; if it ain't, it's not pulling its weight. Excuses. No more excuses.
(and suddenly)
FUCK ME!

> *(and simply launches himself without warning upon MRS AYRTON, who barely has enough time to protect herself. They fight and do a dance macabre of struggle… in a strange silence… until PEEL gets the better of her, gets her face down in the sand and sits on her shoulders. He stares fixedly ahead.*
>
> *In the meantime, this has stirred MOCK from his drunken sleep. He manages to sit up.*
>
> *When he does so, PEEL and MRS AYRTON simply stop fighting. He happens to be sitting on her at the time.*
>
> *Finally, PEEL and MOCK converse. There is little expression in their voices; neither has the energy for much of that…)*

MOCK: An' what would all that be?

PEEL: What would what be?

MOCK: What I was dreaming of, but can't rightly say.

PEEL: Me, I dreamt a thing of the swamp was crawling all over my private part.

MOCK: Is that a way of treating it?

PEEL: The thing of the swamp?
  (intimately, nodding head towards her)
Are we talking of…?

> *(With a burst of energy, MRS AYRTON throws him off her.*
>
> *She stands with her face covered horribly in sand. When PEEL notices it:)*

PEEL: AAGH!

MRS AYRTON: (the usual) PERVERT! LOOKER!

MOCK: (hungover) Steady up, missus.

> *(He rouses himself and performs very crabby ablutions (finger cleaning his teeth etc) not caring that the other two are watching. He is quite evidently now very un-servant-like. Goes to shuffle off his a wave to them of his hand)*

PEEL: Just where do you think you're going?

MOCK: Call me Mokkara, boss-o.

PEEL: I'll call you up to the assizes, that's what I will. So?

(MOCK just stands there, swaying)

MRS AYRTON: Servants of a certain colour these days.

PEEL: (at MOCK) You look like you've been rolling in the mud, fellow.

MOCK: That what her name was, was it?

PEEL: Can she even communicate?

MOCK: Looks like she has her ways.

(He shakily takes out his pad, presumably goes to write some-her's name down)

PEEL: Stop that; you're making the paper shake.

MOCK: (agreeing) Pretty damn noisy too.

PEEL: I'm not meaning that, you fellow. Just be a little mindful of the Peel appearance, n' whatnot.

MOCK: The what?

PEEL: The Peel appearance.

(MOCK writes that down just as shakily; but obviously hasn't finished:)

PEEL: N' whatnot.

MOCK: N' whatnot, rightio.

(He goes to shuffle off again)

PEEL: Stay right where you are!

MOCK: (stopping) The whatnots again?

PEEL: It's not what it looks like.

MOCK: Any whatnot ever are?

PEEL: No whatnot ever is. Look at you. You're a disgrace. That is not *peeling*.

MOCK: Sorry 'bout that.

PEEL: Decorum. Show a little *station*. Did or did we not cart you along for the sole purpose of acting as the colony's interpreter?

MOCK: (again) Rightio.

PEEL: 'Right you are, sir".

MOCK: Right you are, mighty sir. Interpreter. Gotcha.
    (goes to go off, stops, waving pad)
So being that-there interpreter thing, whatnot like… just thought it'd be a good time to improve me English, see. Be a bit much if I turn up at these tribal mobs and say I'm the interpreter an' I got no way of spelling it. What a whatnot that's be. So, see, I'm working hard to improve m'self as the interpreter going about like this. Not easy, it do say, in the pay of a Peel, boss-o… an' ain't that right?

PEEL: You are a silly fellow, Mock. How are those natives going to know what you're even talking about when you're the interpreter, which means they can't speak English in the

73

first place?

MRS AYRTON: (agreeing) Feeble minded!

MOCK: Them tribal mob, they might go, 'this fellah darkie, he can't go-along propa English'. You never knows.
(waves notebook again)
Best to be prepared.

PEEL: (pity-the-poor) Now you're deluding yourself they can read and write, Mock.

MRS AYRTON: Feeble minded, always was!

MOCK: I reckon they can. They're down there givin' lessons to your mob right now, boss-o.

PEEL: (dismissing as nonsense) And what you were saying before: It's pronounced 'proper' and it's 'you never *know*'.

MOCK: (waving his pad) See, it's goin' on improving m'English, mighty sir. No time, I'll know what I'm interpreting to them, you can bet your batting on it.
(looking down at own muddy dishevelled state)
Looks like I started explaining something last night.

(Shudders, then goes to shuffle off)

PEEL: I asked where you think you're going.

MOCK: Start building a house for my family.

PEEL: (to MRS AYRTON) And he hasn't got a family.

MOCK: That's what I just remembered I started explainin' last night. Better go an' finish it.

74

PEEL: She might have strange diseases, fellow!

MOCK: She has now, mighty sir.

(He leaves shakily)

PEEL: (after him) It'll be all sticks and stone!

MOCK: (looking back in) Like the stables you let me have back home, boss-o?

PEEL: Not as good? Of course not as good! I've hung my hat up in those stables! Cheeky bugger! And I'm no 'boss-o'! I'm nobody's 'boss-o'!
    (then to her)
Except yours.

(She snorts such derision that he has to be faced-down.

He inspects the horizons to see if there is anything worth inspecting; finding none he goes back to desultatory playing with cricket bat… so desultatory that, when she silently challenges to face up to her bowling, he shakes his head.

Finally, he sits down and stares at 'his' sun, mutters:)

PEEL: Gathering up the old sirloins. Girding up. Got a gird or two needing scratching…

MRS AYRTON: (eventually) You'll get your death sitting there soaking.

PEEL: It's been raining?

MRS AYRTON: Raining, he asks.

PEEL: There's been clouds?

MRS AYRTON: Clouds, he says.

(He points up at 'his' sun)

PEEL: How's that peeling sunburn of yours?

MRS AYRTON: Sunburn, he says. You promised a land of
milk'n'honey. Some land of sunshine and surf, this is! Not
even the serfs take any notice out here. And I know why.
Even being feeble-minded doesn't show down here! I'm so
sick of it, I don't even know why I calling
    (calls for the habit of it)
MURDERER! RAPE! OGLING!...
    (and)
anymore. So there.

PEEL: Here, you sure about the sunshine?

MRS AYRTON: I won't deny sometimes. But it's got a long
way to go, all the way from England. You swore being on the
other side of the world meant all the sun protection we could
want. You liar, you.
    (and then, of course:)
LIAR! PERVERT! OGLER!

PEEL: (still a bit beaten) Please; someone feeble-minded
enough might hear you.

MRS AYRTON: (bitterly) Nobody cares if I feel better.

PEEL: I think I must be slightly out of whack with a few
things, don't you? Might be a good idea to stop running

76

around trying to do everything and sit here, take a long deep breath, and think for a bit.

MRS AYRTON: Don't do that!

PEEL: (half heartedly) What?

MRS AYRTON: Think! Nobody knows how bad that might be for you down here!
     (then looking closely at his new 'sun reverie')
There, he's gone and done it.

> *(She groans, at a loss of what to do. She puts her gag back on, gets her wrists 'tied' very loosely, and sits back on sand.*
>
> *They are both down at mouth, lifeless:)*

PEEL: Have I tried drowning you lately?

MRS AYRTON: No.

PEEL: Have you tried it yourself lately?

MRS AYRTON: No.

PEEL: Are you sure?

MRS AYRTON: Yes.

PEEL: Not even thought about it?

MRS AYRTON: No.

PEEL: (dully) Everything's a good idea for a think.
MRS AYRTON: It is.

(Blackout)

7.

(Just PEEL and 'his' unerring sun in an otherwise darkened stage.

He comes 'awake' with a jolt of energy, rises with resolve and goes to take a determined step towards it. But, with but one step, he immediately hits an invisible barrier and almost bounces back to where he was.

Still full of manic energy, he turns, launches himself off the piano top and towards the interior.

As soon as he reaches the deep shadow lines, he again hits invisible barriers that he cannot pass beyond)

PEEL: Long way in. Brer Rabbit and the tar baby.
   (that pulls him up short)
What's 'brer rabbit and the tar baby'?

(He shudders, starts to itch badly again, returns defeated back to the piano top)

PEEL: (muttering) How do I know what's brer rabbit and the tar baby? I'm only the 12th man.

(Blackout)

8.
(More than just PEEL snoring. Lighting comes up, as

usual, from 'his' sun and then highlighting him, half asleep and half staring up at it, sitting with his arms on his knees.

As the general lighting comes up, the 'gang' is back sleeping-and-waking around the piano, although MOCK and FRED PEEL are missing.

That time has passed is evident by the beard growth on the men and the tears and general deterioration of the women's dress

A particularly-choked snore from MRS AYRTON brings PEEL back to the present. He rises fairly sprightly and takes up his batting stance at the popping crease.

Obviously a 'wake-up' routine now, MRS AYRTON rises and automatically bowls to him... these are now not much more than dribbles, which he still misses by a mile. But at least he does so with morning-exercising flourishes. And when he has finished, applies a little throat clearing and farting; the farts he waves off over the sea...)

PEEL: Better with a happy smile than letting it leak out. That last one could land back in dear old England singing a song and waving goodbye. Ha ha. Good morning, all!
(then)
A certain brer rabbit and I are getting mighty sick of you lot coming back here putting the disturbs on.

MRS PEEL: (awake enough to be pained) Except our Freddie. Freddie's not here to put any disturbs on!

PEEL: Now, that makes me worry even more for the little bastard.

MRS PEEL: (alarmed) Why?

PEEL: The way he snores he won't be in any polite company. Good way to stop snoring, to be in cut-throat company.

(He makes throat-slashing movement. She has to be comforted... and now openly... by MACQUEEN)

PEEL: I tell you what more putting the disturbs on first thing in the morning… that tongue of his still not caring where your nostrils might have been.
     (then)
Rightio, never mind where the little bastard is, where's Mock?

(Nobody can answer. So he shouts into the interior)

PEEL: Mock? Mock?!
     (even)
Mokkara?!
     (and still to distance; to no one:)
THAT'S MOCK TO YOU!
     (swings around and shouts down the beach)
YOU SEEN M'MAN SERVANT DOWN THERE?
     (still nothing; still shouting:)
SOMEBODY GET A BLOCK AND TACKLE AND LOOK UNDER THOSE LAZY BLOODY WOMEN OF YOURS!

(No MOCK, he has to turn back to his own:)

PEEL: How're I supposed to get my shave?

(This offends MRS AYRTON, who holds up the brush and razor she's been using on him)

MRS AYRTON: I'll have a little appreciation!

PEEL: (dismissive) Both sides. I'm sick of one side a day.

MRS AYRTON: You count your lucky stars, that's what you should do.

PEEL: And only half down the middle. And you clean the razor with a rasp.

MRS AYRTON: You're lucky I don't try to stop *your* snoring with it.

(Now back to grumpy, she self-martyrs herself by – very overtly – getting her gag and her wrist-ties loosely back on. Nobody is even helping her with it now)

PEEL: (by 'his' sun) I can see it's right on twelve, but what we have here is: is it a.m. or p.m.?
   (DORA giggles)
What's makes a rude little harpy from England think it's so funny?

DORA: You are such a fuddy little funny daddy.

PEEL: (ignoring her) I have been considering that bugger Captain Cook again. I wouldn't put it past him not to mention that the Arctic circle down here extends up past the equator or something so obvious to explain why there's twenty-four hour days and twenty-four hour nights. How can you refuse to tell the Admiralty that? I'll tell you how. You're up from the lower-deck, that's how, when other 12th men deserved the promotion instead.
   (at MACQUEEN)
Next time, Lieutenant, when you find the time away from that tongue of yours, take a bearing on it.

MACQUEEN: (now openly slothful) I wouldn't know how.

PEEL: (mimic) 'I wouldn't know how'. Man, you take the
time. You take the sextant. You take a bearing. You take the
time. You've got the time.

HALL: How would he know if it's night or day?

PEEL: ('obvious') You decide if it's night or it's day before
you take the bearing, so shut the cake-hole, you.
    (then)
Is this creature that creature called Hall with his hands on my
daughter, or are they other hands? I know it's you Hall. Get
someone to blow on you and wipe that silly fluff off your face.
No using my razor, either,
    (then, the 'awake' busybody)
Which one was talking so bloody loudly in their sleep?

MRS PEEL: Look who's talking.

PEEL: If you do not know the difference between gnashing
and talking, madam, it was a waste of time the one time in
twenty years we slept together.

MRS PEEL: (mutter, shrug) It *was* a waste of time.

PEEL: I heard that. It might have been a waste of time for
you, but it taught me a lesson I will never forget in life.

MRS PEEL: (for assistance) Mother…?

MRS AYRTON: (now noticeably unhelpful) You married it.

PEEL: (to his daughter) And you tell that creature not to be
so impertinent when he's talking in his sleep.

DORA: (giggling) My papa says not to be so impertinent.

HALL: You didn't say that last night.

DORA: (smutty) Well, you were making me talk so much. I didn't know you had so much elastic.

HALL: Yours ain't too bad neither.

DORA: I saved a few pairs from the wreckage. A gal should never be a physical wreck.

(They chortle between themselves)

PEEL: (to MRS PEEL) Woman, do something about your daughter!

MRS PEEL: I will not.

PEEL: Come again?

MRS PEEL: Well, what do you expect, down here in the Underdone?

PEEL: Bugger me, it's Down Under, not Underdone.

MRS PEEL: Well, she is either one or th'other, and so there! What's the poor girl got to do, but comb her hair? She's become a distinct beach comber, if you must know. It's the Devil's work. All those knots so knotty. Don't I know?

MACQUEEN: (her paramour) Never!

PEEL: You keep your tongue out of this, mister.
    (but has a bright idea)
Eureka Stockade, I have it!

MACQUEEN: (settles for:) No such thing.

PEEL: (stopping) What?

MACQUEEN: No such thing as Eureka Stockade. It's
'Eureka'.

PEEL: I know that.

MACQUEEN: Apparently, you do not.

PEEL: Will you clamp it, man?

MACQUEEN: By God, I'm sick of the clamps, sir!

PEEL: Well, keep…
    (points to his wife)
mum.

MACQUEEN: By God, I will n…
    (stops, realising, changes tack)
Are we all sure?

PEEL: It'll drop off. Just don't say you haven't been warned.
    (and)
Where was I?
    (then resumes his grand idea:)
By Eureka, I have it! This day be Keyboard Day, a
commemoration of waking up to the sights'n'sounds of our
new home!

MRS PEEL: (bitter interpretation) That means the relief
ship's not going to turn up again.

PEEL: Who cares!

(They all shoot their hands up)

PEEL: Nonsense! We have our Keyboard Day!
      (produces paper)
Lucky I thought of a few words before I thought of it.

> *(Imperiously, he gives MRS AYRTON the gee up to get
> to the piano's keyboard. She is totally keen to do so, if
> only to show his dependency on her. She casts off her
> gag etc.*
>
> *But, since the keyboard is by now well buried in the
> sand, she has to look helplessly back at him)*

PEEL: *Dig.* If we've learnt anything it's anything worth
finding down here needs someone to start working the
shovels. Don't scratch the ivories. If we don't find any
tuskers down here, could be worth a bob or two.

> *(Not doubting he has a captive audience, he pays no
> attention to anybody and simply stares up into 'his' sun,
> while she un-earths the keyboard. He turns back only
> when she has done so:)*

PEEL: Play. *Play*. Anything! If it has a strain, it will our
new national anthem!

> *(She strikes the chords. There is no hope that the piano
> will make any sort of recognisable sound. There is just
> a lot of clunking. When, too, she tries to sing a few bars,
> and this is hardly any better.*
>
> *While that may put MRS AYRTON and the others off, it
> does not PEEL. He delivers unctuously his
> commemoration speech, which he reads from the page --*

85

very badly-rehearsed, accompanied by clicking of his
tongue for a cricket ball being struck:)

PEEL: I see a golden sun. Full pelt, it is! And furry? Who knows? Never mind that. There's no run. Halfway on top of the earth upside down we be, out in the centre. And of course the sun will not move. You tell me who said it had to? There's a single to extra cover. New people moving around the new Peel Fold Manor, what? Won't there ever be! Newbies. Revolving orbs. Damn the old northern sun! And there's no run to long on. Realm around and around the realm. Biffing 12th man, that! Nearly just out of this ground, but sense recovered. Wears a cod piece, you know. No new start spread here, eh, haha! Beyond Lords and a good old discreet belch... never hurt anyone... belting the leather off the ball around the back in front of the seventies and over. Taking a single to square leg, good chap. For all that I bring you. Going sweet sweelts svelte sweetly. Oh, I love a sunburnt country lah de dah de dah. Of the top of my England cap. And looking up at the orbulous sky filled with the Big Scoreboard and the moving finger having writ waiting for the next maiden. Going topping century that by the greatest 12th this world has seen. Sir Thomas Peel. Made Sir Thomas for bringing the heavy roller on and now Sir Thomas Peel of Western Australia, postal address to be posted soon. And there are a deft two runs past silly mid-on. Unforgettable for his quote that Man does not a run get, sun or no sun, without the bowel calling for a single, a couple if the first one's run quick ere the flood gates open. The man is the great... pardon the pun!... *colon*-iser who started a great *colon*-y, haha!

(First, MRS PEEL and MACQUEEN take an
opportunity to escape unnoticed)

PEEL: ... Keep thy bat grounded while you're in the runs, Sir Thomas sayeth. Very challenging to the ground staff of the

MCC all this spinifex n' over-lush stuff. Look up into the sun too much and get a southern stroke. Costs a couple more on the scoreboard. Oh, cracking shot down to the third-man boundary by a cracking 12th man! Natural eye in on the sun, don'tee see? Makes keyboards tick over, it do.

(stops, having lost his place. HALL takes the opportunity of:)

HALL: Mr Peel!

PEEL: (not to be stopped now) Drinks called, squash or nuts! Coming soon. First the treats of elements... cf, shade shade shade, hot cracking a hundred before hunch, leg before passing on, hoping the old rain will come, what?, stone-walling on the fences, pinned down, getting to be a nasty curl of the old mo, you know.

HALL: (over him) All the people want is their proper allocation of food n' medicines!

PEEL: (imperial) Give my people all the money they want!

HALL: They don't want any more samples of your handwriting on bits of paper.

PEEL: They'll regret that. Could be worth a lot of money in years to come.

HALL: Not wiped on and buried, they won't.

(PEEL swings around to 'his' sun as if to regather his rhetoric loins.

HALL and DORA give up too, and escape like her mother did with MACQUEEN)

87

PEEL: (back 'on') Yes, yes. All for letting the raff have the riff score and the riff having the raff score. Always a close contest, you know. Fall back on the keyboard. Get used to the light, that's the thing. Only thing is to shoot all the blackbirds or find a way to make them hoarse. A bit of sush around here would be nice. Watch the ball. Could add a verse to the anthem about that. This new springtime country born of a day's play and light going before stumps. Ha to that! Higgle to that! No dawn no day no play no insight none, and its everlasting presence. He sees it as a time of dreams and his eyes light up, and don't ask me who 'he' is. Could be someone called Brer Rabbit. A new dawn clouding out the start of the innings. What can you do but dream-a-time away?

> *(He sees that none, but MRS AYRTON, are left. Which doesn't bother him in the least, while there is still the main camp down the beach)*

PEEL: Hear ye, hear ye, for I know what's in the air will be the air we breathe to which, after this, we will e'er return to!
> *(and blithely carries on, with MRS AYRTON the only audience)*

Head down, bum up, weather the blitz. Blighter of a pitch. In quotes, 'I made that orbless sun move, didn't we all pitch in'. Topping century, that. Sir Thomas Peel. Nice ring to it. No chip off the old block. Uhuh, no. Took new block hold. Laid, saying again, a solid foundation for the innings, what? No 12th man more spiffing. Of Western Australia in knighthood. And there was no run. Sun not moving? Ho ho ho, who cares, says he? And there's another maiden ball. The thing is to keep your back foot grounded and call for drinks before the drought and call for a draught before the floods. Have a nose for it, standing your ground when all around says you're Out. Not being pinned down. Eyes glued on which way's the seam's going.

MRS AYRTON: Oi, who are you talking to?

PEEL: (ignoring her) Lightning lapping between all our curlies. Yep and yes. To call a single. Add one to nothing and nothing to one, you see. Ah, my people, bond yourself to the pitch laid below. Bride yourselves to the growing of wheats on your scoreless graveyards shifts and leave it all to he who waits back in the pavilion with the tray. For now… from today… oh, yes!... I give you your dowry: five hundred working bullocks…

MRS AYRTON: They're all gone!

PEEL: Shut up, will you?
     (and running all together)
… five hundred working bullocks, young, two thousand milch cows heifers and calves two bats three sets of stumps one thousand head of rams and ewes one hundred horses mares and foals included three hundred boars and sows one thousand geese a dozen new balls and six sets of bails one thousand fowls not of the air two hundred turkeys twenty tons of salt beef ten tons of salt pork six pads twenty tons of salt flour cheese and butter ten pairs of batting gloves forty chests of tea and coffee and pepper and Ile de France unmilled sugar four hundred weight of saltpeter plant seeds two outfits of gentlemen creams for the special occasion as of now… oh, good shot, sir!... fruit trees etcetera vines coals bricks etcetera…

     (finally trails off)

MRS AYRTON: I've not seen you open your mouth and say one decent word, but that beats the cake, that does!

PEEL: (last desperate attempt) Free allotments for anyone

who hurrahs!
(gets nothing)
Free leg irons for those what don't!

(MRS AYRTON puts her hand up)

PEEL: *Not you!*

(He manages to re-compose himself; turns to confront 'his' sun and addresses it defiantly)

PEEL: Need to keep one end going, hold out on one's own? What else is new? Always should have been in the first eleven. When in Pal Mall go pell mell, don't you know!
(finally)
Well, that should last until the end of play.

(He gathers his loins, steps off the piano and, followed by MRS AYRTON no matter how many times he tries to brush her off, he strides three time around the piano before, quite incredibly bravely, makes out for the interior.

There, on its dark brink, he stops and cannot go any further. Behind him, 'his' unerring sun beckons him back.

He retreats back to piano)

PEEL: (surly) I want Mock.

MRS AYRTON: (her rival) I heard he turned his coat. He's been rolling around in the mud.

PEEL: He's always rolling around in the poo.

MRS AYRTON: He's been doing it like a native, not like you would.

PEEL: Or you.

MRS AYRTON: I have never rolled around in the mud in my life. Or poo.

PEEL: (chuckles) Good old Mock.
  (and, suddenly overcome)
If I have a little noonday snooze, will you disappear like a bad dream?

> *(She refuses to deign an answer. PEEL lies down under 'his' sun and drops off immediately in its basking.*
>
> *FRED PEEL has obviously been waiting to creep into the camp.*
>
> *He does so, silently gesturing to MRS AYRTON whether he can do so without her raising the alarm to his father. At first, she silently refusing but, on his gestured pleading, she signals he can only do so if he puts back her gag and ties her hands behind her back 'properly'. ... And this time she insists her ankles are tied together.*
>
> *He complies to her wishes.*
>
> *He is in a sorry state that indicates he is having a hard time of it 'interiorly'. Cautiously, he creeps over to a hand mirror, inspects himself, cannot like what he sees.*
>
> *He opens his father's Gladstone bags and removes a waistcoat and jacket and cravat. 'Rescues' also a pair of fairly-polished boots from the sand.*

Save the boots, these he silently puts on, and begins to look quite the toff. The hand mirror tells him satisfactorily so, but MRS AYRTON – disapproving but now really gagged'n'bound hand and foot – at least with her eyes doesn't.

FRED turns, goes to move off, thinks better of it. He returns and has the audacity to actually move onto the top of the piano with PEEL. There, he has the new nerve and impertinence to 'toff-up' an Irish jig, bows, gets off, lifts his leg on the piano like a dog to demonstrate his feeling for his father for her, then jauntily moves off. He is not slinking now; he strides off with head high and shoulders back. A dandy with snuff.

He doesn't really get far...)

PEEL: (one eye open) Hold it right there, you little bastard, you!
    (his son stands caught in headlights)
I know you.

FRED PEEL: (sheepish) I'm your boy, Fred. Fred Peel.

PEEL: You'd want to put up a picket fence around your hut before you build your hut, you do. I hear things.

FRED PEEL: Everybody's doing it, Father. Huts are out.

PEEL: How's my mansion coming along?

FRED PEEL: Fine, fine, Father. I think I heard they think they might have found a proper drawing board. And a ruler. And something to sharpen the pencils. I think they're on the trail of a pencil, even. Real progress.

PEEL: Tell 'em not to forget the piano room.

FRED PEEL: (now backing out) There'll be room for both you and the piano, Father. Maybe not at the same time but one at a time, not to worry.

PEEL: And the cricket pitch? Nobody's allowed to forget the cricket pitch. Or the practice wickets.

FRED PEEL: Last I heard they were debating whether you wanted them laid with peat or wheat.

PEEL: And what did you say?

FRED PEEL: I said toss for it.

PEEL: And you called…?

FRED PEEL: Honestly, Father?

PEEL: Honestly.

FRED PEEL: I can't remember!

PEEL: Idiot! This is important.

FRED PEEL: Well… do they sow peat?

PEEL: Of course they don't sow bloody peat.

FRED PEEL: Then maybe you'll have to use the harvester rather than the roller, Father.

(And then he has slipped away)

PEEL: Where's the right little bastard *going*?

(MRS AYRTON can demonstrate that she can't talk or move much what with her full-on binding and gagging.

Suddenly, PEEL looks – and feels – awfully alone.

Just as suddenly, too, he is having trouble with his right shoulder which now starts the occasional twitch, noticeably towards her.

Maybe because of the difficulty of controlling the twitch, he seems to get another urge to tackle the interior again. But after the usual turns of the piano, he finds MRS AYRTON has shuffled her way to block his path actually heading for the dark interior.

At first it is easy to skirt around her, but, yet again, he cannot get past the edges of the darkness and, when he turns back, he finds it much more difficult to get himself around her. Each time he tries to skirt around her bulk to get back to the piano, his shoulder jabs him with pain.

So, he settles for the bright idea of getting down on his hands and knees and crawling between her straddled legs.

For a full moment he literally disappears.

When he finally manages to emerge, it is with panic and relief of not being totally overwhelmed)

PEEL: Gawd! No 12th man should be subjected to a sight like that!

(He grabs one of her ankles, proceeds to untie it, even though, by starting so, his shoulder renews its stabbing

94

pain. As he does so:)

PEEL: If we don't get some air in here, this colony won't be fit for human habitation.

(MRS AYRTON, of course, is not cooperating. She does not open her legs in any sort of relief when he gets one ankle freed.

Instead, as soon as he does so and even though she is fully and properly gagged, there is an over-arching scream. He quickly 'closes' the ankle back again. The scream stops. Slowly, he 'opens' her legs again. As soon as he does so, there is another scream in the air. He 'closes' the leg again frantically. Tries 'opening' them again. The same scream result each time.

His shoulder is stabbing pain.

He reels back from the whole useless enterprise.

The trouble is that, when he leaves off, the over-arching scream now persists… 'his' unerring sun, returned, pulsing to it… such that he has to cover his ears – and when even this proves ineffective, he throws himself beneath her skirts once more.

Immediately, silence. Calm restored.

Certainly, MRS AYRTON now has a secretive smile on her face.

This time it takes much longer for him to come crawling back out again. He is now beneath her smirk of victory, can only crawl back towards the sanctity of the piano.

But, before he gets there, he is attacked by yet another bout of scratching which he can only get at with his left hand since his right shoulder has temporarily 'gone'. At the end of it, he is a cowled mess, can only lie prone and panting, even if he is not yet totally defeated and can croakily:)

PEEL: Now I know where all the sand flies came out of.

(She gives him the finger as best she can. He goes into a whining justification at his ineffectiveness:)

PEEL: Arm, you know. Was the shoulder. Shoulder arms at the area, sort of. Shoulder arms at the brute of a bouncer's best, see. Small hint of a signal from the pavilion.

(Yet despite this, his arm takes on a life of its own all of a sudden.

Despite any attempt by him to hold it back, it begins edging towards MRS AYRTON – who is in no way trying to avoid it -- as if it has a mind of its own.

Not only is it edging mindlessly towards her but is grabbing for her with the fingers going symbolically 'c'here, c'here'.

It needs a great presence of will for him not to 'go with' it.

Finally, he manages to tear his arm away back 'into its socket'.

He drops back panting, scurries backwards to – now – the refuge within the glare of 'his' sun, where he cries out and up:)

PEEL: My arm's gone sick in the head!

*(A ridiculing snigger breaks out all around. He swings
around guiltily, but there is no one except her there…
and she certainly isn't laughing.*

*The snigger extends to all sides, insinuating and
unhealthy. He blocks his ears miserably.*

Blackout)

ACT 3

9.

(Silence and stillness around PEEL and MRS AYRTON.

She is still gagged and is now bound to a stake as far off from the piano as he dares make it. This has not improved her demeanor. Whether she is sitting or standing there, she stares sourly and contemptuously at him.

He himself is pretending to be silently communicating with 'his' sun, but is obviously making a conscious effort of will not to admit her presence to himself.

He has his whole arm in a sling and this he holds as though it is giving him great pain... which it metaphorically is... but, in truth, is endeavouring to hold it down from doing what it likes.

As though by way of atonement, every now and again it scratches his 'good' arm. But, though in a tight sling, the arm still keeps jerking out grabbingly towards her from time to time. It has obviously become an affliction he can barely bear.

In an attempt to distract himself, he counts very determinedly to ten, then takes a sun bearing through the V-fingers of his good hand. 'His' sun clearly has not moved.

Irritably he swivels around so his back is towards the sun and counts deliberately – but, in an attempt at being cunning, under his breath -- to ten again.

*He swings around to it suddenly and takes a 'quickie'
new bearing on it. But it has not moved... at least he is
not quick enough to catch it moving.*

*He gives up, tries to ignore her through idleness but
finds it infuriatingly impossible to do while his arm
keeps up the occasional grabbing give-me, give-me grab
towards her.*

*Under muffle she gives him what-for each time his arm
tries it and each time he reels his gimme, gimme fingers
back in.)*

PEEL: (a hexing sign at her) Stop trying to encourage it!
      (she shakes her head)
You are!
      (she shakes her head)
You are!
      (then, outcry)
WHY DOES THIS PLACE HAVE TO BE SUCH AN
UNPERFECT PUFF?

*(She muffle-sniggers again; and quite blandly hops over
to be near enough to him that he can, as she indicates she
wants, untie her, save for the gag which she allows to
remain for the time being.*

*While he does this absent-mindedly – and between
scratching; trying to control his arm now that she is
tantalizingly closer – he endeavours to regain the 'old'
Peel with out-loud bombast to no one except her and 'his'
sun really.*

*For this, he rips out scraps of paper and reads randomly
from them. He begins okay but fast starts to lose any
energy he has been able to muster:)*

PEEL: By all that's holy I've written here that Marco Polo wasn't saddled with his mother-in-law. No way. Nor was Columbus. Not even that bloody Captain, haha what a laugh, Cook and if that bugger didn't have such a mother fixation we might have been able to block things out. Four rings, give him? They should've extracted his one ring with their digits! What did I do to deserve it?

(spits)

Cook! Him getting into the gentlemen's clubs and thinking I'd believe him by coming all the way out here when I've got 12th-man obligations, you know. Twelfth-man. It was a real off day when I got roped down n' hitched. Real grubber; hardly rose from the pitch.

(arm pain)

Uh.

(has to fight holding it in from reaching for her, and:)

Here's the thing… See? What's the thing?

(at her)

Your fault, witch.

(He breaks into a patriotic 'Men of Harlech' and, while doing so, steps off piano to stride martially around the piano, breaking past her rudely and, on the surface of it, disdainfully. [His arm wants to linger; get pulled along with him.]

But he soon runs down again, only manages to get back 'onto his box' on the piano under 'his' sun again, and continue reading from his scraps of paper:)

PEEL: All apparently succumbed. Yours truly standing tall like any honourable 12th man should. This place swallowed 'em all up. Chomp chomp. Don't expect much I told the parliamentary committee. Give me as much time as I need to absorb. Must be a bloody lot more land than you mean

sods're going to grant me. Didn't I? On the chompers. Sink
the teeth in down here rather than trying to change the odd
pound or two in France. What frogs! I've always said, the
thing is to run your fingers down the seam.

MRS AYRTON: Seams?

PEEL: (defiantly) Seams, seams!

MRS AYRTON: You leave my seams out of it, you!
    (and of course automatically goes off into:)
MURDER! RAPE! LOOKING!

        (which is now no longer phasing him at all. In fact:)

PEEL: You stoat. You sour cow. You milkless boil. You
titless wonder. Flap off. Cunny off. Broom off. Buzz off.
Bugger away. Leave a man bee bee bee.
    (stops to suddenly whine at her)
Listen, if I free your mouth before that gag is never going to
be the same again, will you promise you won't raise the roof?
    (she looks pointedly upwards; 'what roof?')
Well, when we get the best roof you've ever seen, anyway.
Not that any roof'd do you any good, what with you being
born with that hole in your head. So, promise…?

        *(She won't commit herself. She wants him to
        symbolically to fully untie the gag around her neck. He
        knows this, as much as she does. It is he who gives in
        first to make the first move towards her, but when he
        reaches to free the cloth his arm flies into its gimme,
        gimme at her sexual parts again.*

        He has to fight this frantically.

        Morally on top, she removes the gag herself, but leaves

101

it dangling as a symbol that it is there to be used to control him again. Nor is she about to let him off the hook now that she has him there; despite the fact it is she who has been edging closer to him:)

MRS AYRTON: You just keep that crabby fore finger thing off me!
(he desperately fights his fore finger)
You keep that crabby middle finger thing off me!
(he desperately fights his middle finger)
Just keep that crabby ring finger thing off me!
(he desperately fights his ring finger)
You keep that crabby little finger off me!
(he desperately fights his little finger and only gets the contempt of:)
I'm not talking of those crabby finger things. I'm talking about that crabby thumb thing!

PEEL: (near defeat now) These fingers have been sweating away in a batting glove, that's all.

MRS AYRTON: Yes, and now they have the cheek to think I am some old bat to hold.
(and gives him both barrels:)
PERVERT! LOOKER!

PEEL: (matching her) HOW LONELY AND DESPERATE CAN A POOR MAN GET?!

(It is just about his all for now. She is literally standing over him while the unerring sun noticeably fades a lot)

MRS AYRTON: Admit you're a sorry sight.

PEEL: (but weakly) No.

102

MRS AYRTON: Admit they've all abandoned you.

PEEL: No.

MRS AYRTON: You tried to drown me.

PEEL: I will admit I got a duck there.

MRS AYRTON: And don't you ever say you'll keep my civil tongue in a preserving jar again! Or that I smell like I've got gangrene! I know what I smell like and it's nowhere near gangrene. Look where you've brought us to! If I wanted a gutter I could have rolled over and gone back to sleep in London.

> *(Deliberately she steps towards him to provoke his arm, which reacts yeah-yeah. She steps back.*
>
> *She steps near him again. Same reaction from arm. She steps back)*

MRS AYRTON: (not without pleasure) I told my little Dorie. I said look out for the lack of moral fibre what's before your eyes.

PEEL: (miserably) I can build you a gutter here.

MRS AYRTON: Murderer! Pervert!

> *(But her heart really isn't in it.*
>
> *Now crushed, he sits under 'his' sun and hides his face in his arms.*
>
> *In turn, now victorious, she idles about making gestures of doing basic chores.*

103

Long pause, before:

FRED PEEL swings in as wide-a-boy as any wide-boy could be. He is now outfitted gaudily in his oversized father's clothes, but is now sporting a large bowtie and sleeve garters straight out of vaudeville, together with a snake-oil salesman's tartan tote bag)

FRED PEEL: I say I say I say… what did the explorer say to the eunuch?
 (and)
'Doctored living stones', I presume?' Ha ha. Here's another: What did the snake-oil salesman say to the snake? 'Bend over; this won't slither a bit'!   Oh I say I say I say. Difficult audience tonight! Why did the chicken cross the road? Because he was no chicken! Nobody laugh until it hurts! And so hello and goodbysies…!

(He turns to leave again by:)

MRS AYRTON: Hey, you. I think he wants you.

(She indicates PEEL who is feebly holding his 'bad' arm up for attention – for which FRED PEEL flourishingly obliges)

FRED PEEL: What did the snake-oil salesman says to the snake number two? 'Don't coil me, I'll coil you!'   Oh, wot a wit! It only hurts when I rub it in, guv.

PEEL: (very dully) Who are you, apart from my real little bastard idiot son?

FRED PEEL: (perfunctorily takes up 'bad' arm) Dr Dio Doodle come a-diddling as good as they come.

MRS AYRTON: That diddling's his trouble. Not as bad as *ogling* yet, though.

FRED PEEL: I see, I see. Hmm and hmm as we hmming go.

(He proceeds to do a clownish medical examination of the offending arm, using manipulations and a reflex hammer and stethoscope.

While he does so, MRS AYRTON pipes up, the bedside visitor:)

MRS AYRTON: I can perhaps forgive him for saying all pack up we're going for a little trip around the Isle of Wight and it was halfway around the world not the Isle of Wight. I can forgive him for him for slapping me in irons half a mile outside of Portsmouth. I can forgive him for trying to get me to step off at Africa when Africa was five miles off the starboard bow. I can forgive him for loading stores on me when we arrived and saying sorry he thought I was a whaler when I was already loaded with crew. But I cannot and will not forgive him for that cartoon they did of him in *Punch* showing him plucking a poor white swan. And no asking why I won't forgive him. I have no idea why, so it proves it's his fault right down to the core.

FRED PEEL: (re the arm) I say I say, what's wrong with this arm, did anyone say?

PEEL: It wants to grab her.

FRED PEEL: My God, it's serious!
    (pinches the arm)
Feel that?
    (PEEL shakes his head)

By God, sir, your arm's gone numb!

PEEL: What arm?

FRED PEEL: (at his left arm) Your right arm!

PEEL: That's not right!

FRED PEEL: I know it's not, sir.

PEEL: That's my left!

FRED PEEL: I say I say, don't tell me it's in the left too!

PEEL: No.

FRED PEEL: Well, that can't be right!
      (produces saw-bones' saw)
Stand back, I say!

PEEL: No!

FRED PEEL: Better left?

PEEL: Yes.

FRED PEEL: Better right left?

PEEL: No! Yes!

FRED PEEL: But enough of these pleasantries! Did someone
call to the sidelines about an arm? More importantly than the
poisons within is, I say I say I say, what did the nanny goat
say to Billy?
      (blows toy horn)
'Are you kidding me?', haha. There's more from where that

came from… what is a humble fellow with one foot in the grave and one foot in his mouth? Why, sir, he has gone to 's grave tongue-tied to the last!
(and)
They just keep pouring out.
(and turns attention back to the arm)
Let's see if it's got one of them wills of its own.

(He lets the arm 'go' and, so freed, shoots out rigidly towards MRS AYRTON with greater determination than before)

FRED PEEL: That's a neat trick.

(PEEL dry retches on what now seems an inevitability)

FRED PEEL: That's the ticket, sir. Avoid the self-abuse. Or take one of my remedies, ha ha. Deal with the likes of this all the time in my trade. Arms like this have no sense of proportion, never have. It's them idle hands, sir. Open drawers an' they're shootin' in there like a shot.

PEEL: (stopping) What sort of shot?

FRED PEEL: Back cut, I'd say, mostly.

PEEL: Sneaky things, back cuts. Too much of a risk. Never advocated 'em.

FRED PEEL: Nothing quicker on the drawers, no. Drains the dignity right out of the armpits, these sorts of arms do. Sorry to see n' sorry to say.
(then)
Say aah.

PEEL: Aah.

FRED PEEL: Cough.
    (PEEL does so)
Again.
    (again, PEEL does so)
Ooo, bit nasty that. The devil's work, this is. Say ninety-nine.

PEEL: Ninety-nine.

FRED PEEL: 'Undred.

PEEL: Hundred.

FRED PEEL: Don't care…

PEEL: Don't care…

FRED PEEL: if I do go blind.

PEEL: if I do go blind.

FRED PEEL: Any better now?

PEEL: A bit.

FRED PEEL: Next thing you'll be up and guessing the time.
Turn around please.
    (PEEL does so)
Now let it have its head.

> *(He steps quickly back while, though PEEL is now*
> *facing away from MRS AYRTON, his arm shoots*
> *backwards to starting grabbing directly at her.*
>
> *FRED PEEL plunges a vaudeville needle into it.)*

108

PEEL: Ow!

FRED PEEL: Ah, you felt that, did you?

PEEL: No.

FRED PEEL: Why did you say 'ow' for?

PEEL: ('simple') I saw you do it.

FRED PEEL: Oh well, that's a good sign. Still in the land of the living. Laugh.

PEEL: I will not.

FRED PEEL: Prey, why not? Said the spider to the fly.

PEEL: It only hurts when I laugh.

> *(FRED pulls out a toy trumpet, blows fanfare to punchline. But gravely continues diagnosis:)*

FRED PEEL: Hmm, how's the old urine?

PEEL: Clear-eyed.

FRED PEEL: (conclusion) In that case, that settles it! Sir and Madam, this 'ere arm be numb!
   (to their doubtful looks)
Nay, I go further and speccy that this 'ere arm is your bowling arm.

PEEL: The first googly known to a 12th man!

FRED PEEL: Of course. Now close your eyes, sir.

(PEEL does so. FRED PEEL pulls out a wooden hammer again, tests the elbow's reflexes. When he does so, the opposite leg shoots out. He tests the reflexes of the other elbow. The other opposite leg shoots out. He tests the left knee and the right arm shoots out. Tests the right knee and the left arm shoots out)

FRED PEEL: Interesting.

MRS AYRTON: What's interesting about it?

(FRED PEEL paces up and down, rubbing his chin, then turns back to PEEL)

FRED PEEL: I say I say I say. Sir, that arm ain't numb. That there arm's…
(blows trumpet)
frustrated!

PEEL: What do you mean 'frustrated'?

FRED PEEL: Why, not connected, sir! Feeling out of joint, like. Not where it wants to go. Simple.

PEEL: No!

FRED PEEL: See it all the time once an arm's past a certain ailing stage, sir.
(clownishly trying to comfort him)
Like I says, the Devil's own work, sir. The Only Thing Left to Fiddle With, all in capital letters! In towns too. In villages. Camps. Cubbyholes and in corners. Oh, sir, in creeks or creaky beds. The Devil, He got dat arm!
(whispers)
Self-abuse of the person, sir. Terrible to see. Wails of gnashing anguishes. Sir, sir…

110

(fiercer whisper)
the great grope gggrrr-nashingly groped for!

> *(PEEL falls on his knees before 'his' unerring sun,*
> *ululates his agony up at it:)*

PEEL: UN-NUMB ME!

> *(But its light begins to fade from him, as does the*
> *general lighting… and FRED PEEL backs out and away*
> *with:)*

FRED PEEL: Not alone, sir, no. Even seen worse by way of…
> *(meaning MRS AYRTON)*
the object of desire. Only last week, yours truly married a schizzo-friendly-ack person to 'imself. Couldn't take his hands off 'imself, that one. Him too, lonely in his universe, piteous for companionship, like your poor arm there, sir. I said to him, do you take this self of yours until death do you part and he goes all 'Yes!'. That's hope and optimism for you right there, that is… Toodleloo.

> *(Fade, all, to blackout)*

10.
(A slow uptake of overall lighting coming onto the piano camp.

As the lighting comes up, the voice of MRS AYRTON grows over all. She starts it unseen and ends in full light:)

MRS AYRTON: (mainly voice over) I don't mind saying

I'm talking to myself. I do it eggerly! Here, I eggerly do. Back where I used to so eggerly call home, eggs were the things what came in from out of the muck and let you use the silver spoons. I like using the silver spoons back then. I was egger to! But here I don't mind calling it home. Egger it is. You can tell by the rain dust what husks in eggerly to the shore here it's a home of eggs all around so googy so good! All eggs, all eggerlies. They say I could lay eggs here. I am! Behind every rock, don'tee know, there a spirit child egger to pick you out an' jump into your belly or there's one of your own kind of spirit women all behind every rock egger to egg you on and on, go on n' egg all over! They say here even the snakes and the lizards 'round here lay eggs. Even the spiders'n'slime-ers 'round here lay eggs. Everything's doing it eggerly 'round here. They are! Even them large bits, eggs. Even those things they eggly call kangaroos hopping 'round here looking for their lost eggs, on the hop, egger not to tread them underfoot. All the local women, eggs in their bellies, out from behind them rocks and bushes. Oh, yes. Even them damn sand flies 'round here are egger to lay their eggs on my steaming parts. I don't mind. Egg on, I say. I try to tell that pervert of a man, u-kno-who, call it Eggland. New Eggland, I don't care. Doesn't matter if it's north, south, east or west. Just get the egg part in. It's my eggerness. It's my eggerly home. He won't, will he? The egghead. This is what I think anyway.

(The piano camp is now fully lit, where she and PEEL haven't changed or seemed to have moved much.

She is free of gag etc now, is quite 'eagerly/eggerly' doing chores about the place. He is sitting in his familiar place, familiarly with hands on knees looking up at 'his' sun... or at least, where 'his' sun used to be.

It is not there now.

Now he is waiting for it to come back.

His offending arm is even more haltered by a sling, but, even so, it occasionally 'escapes' to fling itself at her... especially when her female parts come close enough to be within striking distance.

To be with them comes MACQUEEN. He is idle there, as though he could find no duties to do inland and has wandered in there.

MRS AYRTON addresses PEEL's lassitude:)

MRS ARYTON: The doctor left you with plenty to go on with.

PEEL: He was no doctor.

MRS ARYTON: Well, he prescribed prayer, so he had to be a doctor.

PEEL: I haven't built the church yet!

MRS AYRTON: You don't need a church to pray.

(PEEL gives her a withering look)

PEEL: Oh, you don't, do you?

(but it is pretty obvious she doesn't take much notice of him now)

MRS AYRTON: (shrugs) I've heard that. Just saying.

PEEL: You listening to all the treasonable things being

113

bandied around.

(to her 'so what' shrug)
Without the bounce of four walls, where do you think God's god almighty answers would end up?

MRS AYRTON: Out to sea?

PEEL: ('yes') Out to sea.

MRS AYRTON: Or not.

PEEL: Don't be ridiculous. They'd be out there on their way to China.

MACQUEEN: (trying to be helpful) Have you tried him with cold baths?

MRS AYRTON: Him? Baths?

PEEL: (pointing out to sea) You try bathing in there, you'll get your bum bitten off.

MRS AYRTON: We're only trying to help.

PEEL: *Where's it gone?*

> *(But as much as he agonizes over just an unlit spot in the sky where 'his' sun used to be, nothing will bring it back.*
>
> *Even MRS AYRTON, in a fit of sympathy, moves up to be close behind him... she protects herself from his frantically twitching arm given her close proximity... peers over his shoulder sighting the sky where he is looking, but can't see or work out what he is looking for.*

She straightens and pointedly shrugs 'beats me' to
MACQUEEN who doesn't the same back to her)

MACQUEEN: (trying to be helpful) We only lost one more and that was a few weeks ago.

(PEEL doesn't deign to query it, but she is curious enough to raise her eyebrows)

MACQUEEN: (explanation) Bathing wise. But that was a little girl a long, long way off from being productive.

MRS AYRTON: That's not very nice to know.

MACQUEEN: (finally pipes up) There was Saint Magnus. I think. Much dipping of the genitals in icy water. Sort of thing. Too. Probably used to gag a lot.

MRS AYRTON: (re PEEL) He still says it's only his arm.

MACQUEEN: Well, genitals ain't too far away from arms.

MRS AYRTON: That's true.

PEEL: (justifying himself) Exercise, he said. Defeat the Devil's purpose with exhaustion. Flagellation.
    (bitterly)
I'm stuck with her. Who needs flagellations.

MRS AYRTON: See what I have to put up with?

PEEL: (whine) I'm a sufferer from hay fever, you know.

(Pause.

PEEL returns to mentally trying to coax 'his' sun back)
115

PEEL: The count of sixty precision seconds done very precisely. Forward block, bat straight, elbow up. An exact moment of a minute of astrophysical precision unerringly homing in to the middle peg. Stop; take elevation. Verify elevation. No more than sixty or taken off for wasting time. Employ navigation. Consider all variables. Multiple by the constant k, being the speed of a very good yorker.

> *(During this, MACQUEEN has got up and is leaning over his shoulder sighting where PEEL is looking, as MRS AYRTON had done earlier.*
>
> *PEEL sensing his presence, daringly on the piano top, and looks back and down with contempt until MACQUEEN backs off to the sand... nothing will ever change it seems... yet MACQUEEN remains curious:)*

MACQUEEN: (re missing 'sun') No go?

PEEL: (above it) That is a very colloquial expression. What next with that mouth of yours.

MACQUEEN: (shrugs) No dice?

PEEL: Please, speak English. And, no.

> *(But MACQUEEN is now all bent to help out with the missing 'sun')*

MACQUEEN: Want me to have a go?

PEEL: Quite unthinkable.

MRS AYRTON: Go on. He's just sticky today.

(which makes PEEL very surly… but noticeably not protesting her and, anyway, MACQUEEN is still pressing to be helpful:)

MACQUEEN: Tried 'tick tock'?

PEEL: Make sense, man.

MACQUEEN: Not tried 'tick tock' eh? At sea, m'commander always had us go 'tick tock' when something up there's gone missing. Like the last sun bearing. Never fails.
       (to PEEL's renewed hope, urgingly:)
'Tick tock'.

(PEEL sights along his good arm to where 'his' sun was, and:)

PEEL: Tick tock.

MACQUEEN: I found it best with more feeling in it, personal like.

PEEL: Tick tock!

MACQUEEN: Try this then.

(PEEL allows MACQUEEN to get back on piano, sight sky over his shoulder and do magical word-and-gesture nonsense:)

MACQUEEN: Hooley hooley hooley dooley…!

(Instantly, the unerring sun flickers in the sky, but just as quickly dies down)

117

PEEL: You see that?!

MACQUEEN: Definitely.
   (then)
See what?

   (Quickly, PEEL tries)

PEEL: Hooley hooley…

   (but nothing)

MACQUEEN: (encouragingly) … hooley dooley.

PEEL: Hooley hooley hooley dooley!

   (but still gets absolutely nothing. He grabs MACQUEEN by the jacket to do it again)

PEEL: Again!

MACQUEEN: Hooley…

   (the sun starts flickering again. PEEL pushes him aside:)

PEEL: … *hooley hooley dooley!*

   (But 'his' sun has gone again.

   He waits in vain, and then sudden loses all patience with it, raves up at it:)

PEEL: Ticktockticktockticktock!

   (The sun suddenly bursts into activity. It not only

118

instantly appears but starts motoring across the sky. At first PEEL is jubilant, follows its passage in pointing exaltation:)

PEEL: Midday. Evening. Night. Dawn. Midday. Evening.
(as it speeds up)
Nightdawnmidday…!
(until)
STOP! TOO FAST!

> *(It apparently does so, on demand. But it then quickly and totally disappears again. For a moment he is even mightily relieved)*

PEEL: I've aged a month already.

> *(He looks up for it again now that he has regained his breath. But he seems to sense that it has now gone forever. His renewed 'ticktockticktock' to bring it back is hardly even audible. Finally, he gives up, hangs his head in his one good hand)*

PEEL: Gone. All gone.

> *(Pause, not unsympathetic to him)*

MRS AYRTON: Something gets into his mind, he won't give up, I'll say that. Specially something perverted.

MACQUEEN: (aside to her) He tried 'the rain in Spain falls mainly on the plain' before his time?

MRS AYRTON: (ditto, nodding) First off.

> *(With a brave effort, PEEL has rallied himself to show he has leadership quality)*

119

PEEL: (into air) Right, you lot. All present? Recovered?
Nasty near shipwreck that was, I grant ee. Still, told we didn't
lose too many. First landfall we wouldn't want to fall too
much in numbers, eh?, ha ha. But character building. Never
forget that. Tell your grandchildren one day. 'Mr Peel, he
started us off character building'. So, right, let's 'ave yer! I
said to the parliamentary committee I said I'll call it the New
Start, and by God that's what it is! New Start. Coined it
m'self. Here cometh the proper Western Australia! Be the
first over those-there sandhills and remember England expects
every contractee to do his duty to the contractors!

*(He stops for something but can't seem to remember
what)*

PEEL: (sourly at MACQUEEN) What've you turned up back
here for anyway?

MACQUEEN: Just got to wondering what the tally is here?

PEEL: And about time too. Well, we've been here a month…

MACQUEEN: Twelve.

*(PEEL stares at him as though he is crazy, but carries
on:)*

PEEL: … Adjutant General and you can't count up to thirty
or thirty-one days?

MACQUEEN: (cheerfully) No blessed idea.

MRS AYRTON: (dealing with idiots) He's meaning months
not days.

120

PEEL: (reeling them off) Four hundred men, give or take a 'undred or so, woman and children, all snotty-nosed brats. Common labourers, ploughmen, carpenters, gardeners, thatchers, sawyers, joiners, wheelwrights, blacksmiths, and the full ingredients of the First Eleven of the Peel Fold Manor Cricket Club under Royal patronage.
    (stops, looks around, sees nothing)
All got nearly eaten alive, you know. Had to leave the beach. Quite puss-y, really. Cowards!

> *(He waits, but just gets an ironic tip of the forelock from MACQEEN who simply departs)*

MACQUEEN: Rightio, thanks. I'll have a good long think on what we've just said.

> *(Abandoned, PEEL turns accusatorily to MRS AYRTON)*

PEEL: I need two good arms to carry out my mission, but you don't care!

MRS AYRTON: (sarcastically) I *eggerly* await your next move.

> *(and with equal sarcasm steps closer to him and watches amused as he struggles – barely successfully – to control his arm. She steps back, point made)*

PEEL: *I've got to get on.*

MRS AYRTON: (flatly) Right.
    (and taunting)
Tick tock.

PEEL: (desperately hopeful back up at missing sun) Ticktockticktockticktock!

MRS AYRTON: Tried 'tock tick'?

(He knows when the taunting has become beyond the family pale)

PEEL: Give me my arm back!

(She can only snigger. And then for fun:)

MRS AYRTON: OGLER! PERVERT! MURDER HERE!

(Blackout)

11.

(Lighting back on PEEL and MRS AYRTON. He is sitting forlornly. She is busying herself, very ostensibly and loudly, with basic easy chores.

'His' sky is empty still.

He is having a tormented time of it now… not so much with scratching the sand-fly bites, but with his head and his left arm. His head seems to have a mind of his own too, looking repeatedly up at the sky for 'his' sun to come back. His left arm is giving him even more trouble as she draws near; as such times, she growls a warning:)

MRS AYRTON: Ten-foot pole, ten-foot pole…

(PEEL's helplessness with himself is at least relieved by the entry of MOCK.

MOCK has gone native. There are only the vestiges of his English livery left on him. His hair is wild and he has a few body-scarring 'tattoos'.

He comes back into the camp perfunctorily, now not really paying even lip service to his duties towards PEEL. He plonks himself down under the very-welcoming eye of PEEL and the disapproving eye of MRS AYRTON after she is sure he is indeed MOCK.

Finally:)

PEEL: Mock!

MOCK: Yeah?

PEEL: Old Mock!

MOCK: Anything to wet a whistle?

(To her utter disapproval, PEEL gladly gets up and takes him a flask)

PEEL: (chuckle) Still rolling in that mud, eh? That's my Mock.

MOCK: (correcting) Mokkara.

PEEL: (nodding, but still) That's my Mock.

MOCK: Yeah.

PEEL: How's that roof coming along?

MOCK: What roof might that be?

PEEL: You went off to put a roof over your new family.

MOCK: (shrugging) Dunno about that. Still goin' on getting the families to worry about how many roofs yet.
(then)
Crook arm, eh?

PEEL: (self-disparaging) My leftie seems to have a fatal attraction to…
(re a tongue-clicking MRS AYRTON)
an absolute disaster.

MOCK: (nodding) They drop you?

PEEL: Twelfth man? Never!

MOCK: (sarcastically) Yeah, that'd be right.

(PEEL inspects the new cicatrices on MOCK's arm)

PEEL: See you've got a few new designs y'self. Any I might use for my new coat of arms?
(and)
And how's the interpreting going?

MOCK: Can't understand a word the blighters're saying.

PEEL: You'll get the hang of it. There's thousands of years struggling to get out of the glotturals before we came along, don't you know. Even you.

MOCK: No, not my mob, boss-o. M'trouble is not understanding a blessed word of your mob. Where'd you dig 'em up from?

PEEL: All handpicked from the best of English slums, Mock, you know that. Each one better than you, as appropriate.

MOCK: Rum.

MRS AYRTON: (censorial) We have no rum.

MOCK: (not meaning that) Them's better'n I were?

PEEL: They 'were' not 'was'.

MOCK: (shaking head) Rum, that.

MRS AYRTON: I'll have your mind off rum around here, thank you, mister.

MOCK: (to PEEL) She still kickin' on?
      (to PEEL's crestfallen yes)
No wonder you're losing your hair.

PEEL: I am not. I am trimming down for the battles ahead. Important innings. Long, lonely journey, that getting out into the middle without tripping over. Everybody watching you closely, you know. And all my people are your betters, if you'll remember how I trained you.

MOCK: I tell 'e what's better.
      (giving way to scratching himself)
These English fleas of theirs. Our local ones've all lodged complaints.

      (He sees a group of tribal people coming before they see him)

MOCK: (long suffering) Don't tell 'em I'm here. They won't understand a word.

125

(The shadows of the Aborigines stop at the lighting/shore's edge. They stand very still as threatening shadows.

MRS AYRTON is terrified, dashes to be 'behind' PEEL even if it means climbing onto piano and resisting his occasional shoves to push her off – and slapping down his 'bad' arm when necessary.

PEEL actually shows he is bullish before their threat but also that this only comes from his feeling colonially superior)

PEEL: Off with you.

(But of course they don't move.

PEEL snaps his fingers as though they were a figment of the imagination to be dispatched but finds that not even his accompanying...)

PEEL: Tick tock tick tock.

(... at them will make them go away. He has to revert to MOCK:)

PEEL: Guests of yours? Bit thick, are they?

MOCK: (back to being man-servant) Watch out for them, mighty sir.

PEEL: Have they any idea of how we are hundreds strong and dangerous when badly stung?

MOCK: Dangerous? Them settlers of yours've skirted right

around them, they did.

PEEL: Tell 'em stores purchases is
  (pointing way off)
that way. You're family.

MOCK: I've told 'em that. They say I've made enough
families with them, 's well.

PEEL: (shouting) We have nothing here!
  (back to the other)
Tell 'em the only thing worth saving here is our skins, and
even those burn up n' go all itchy very badly!

MOCK: Not here for that.

PEEL: (outcry) Spare our womenfolk!

  (MOCK looks incredulously at him as to how ridiculous
  that is, to MRS AYRTON's outrage)

PEEL: (acknowledging that to being silly) What do they
want then?

MOCK: We... you... got a spare historian or that-there
'whatnot' of yours? Can't remember.

PEEL: Come again?

MOCK: Told you, they feel skirted around like nobody wants
'em. They're demanding to be put in the picture.

PEEL: They'll go in the picture! I'll make sure they get a
pictorial line or two!

MOCK: (calling out to them) He'll make sure you'll get a

127

pictorial line or two!
(back to PEEL)
Some English they understand.

(The tribals seem to consult amongst themselves)

MRS AYRTON: What, what?

MOCK: (shrugging) They want a 'istorical picture painted of a few spears sticking out of you two.

MRS AYRTON: MURDER! RAPE!

(MOCK quietens her, and then quickly appeases the tribal people with:)

MOCK: 'Ere, mates, the rape's easily denied! Look at her!

(It seems to satisfy the locals. They depart as shadowly as they arrived.

PEEL, MOCK and MRS AYRTON return to what they were doing... PEEL back to silently 'tick-tock'ing up at his missing sun)

MOCK: (can't sleep, re sky) You still on about that?

PEEL: (inconsolable) I've lost something.

MOCK: No good, that. Never get to start a family without that.

(PEEL goes forlornly back to sit facing 'his' missing sun)

PEEL: Tick tock tick tock.

*(MOCK regards him for a while, then gives up on him.
Not being able to settle again, he finally gets up to
leave, but PEEL is sharp to it, and:)*

PEEL: What about all those spears sticking out of me?

MOCK: ('won't happen') I'll just tell 'em you won't return
any spears found in you.

MRS AYRTON: And me.

MOCK: And you. Any that'd stick.

PEEL: Tell them they'd have to put in a chitty for them.

MOCK: ('yeah, yeah') That'll do it.

> *(As he leaves, he bumps into MACQUEEN who is, at
> that time, entering.*
>
> *They meet face-to-face, chest-to-chest as competitors
> and they quite simply start bouncing off each other time
> after time like pinballs.*
>
> *As they repeatedly do so, PEEL raises an inquiring
> eyebrow to her)*

MRS AYRTON: (shrugs) The rumour is they keep running
into each other all over the place.

PEEL: (back up at empty sky) Ticktockticktock…
      (then back to her)
Missus, you ever feel like just… you know… blinking away a
few years?

MRS AYRTON: I do.

PEEL: ('okay') You first then.

MRS AYRTON: After you.

PEEL: All together then… Blink, blink.

MRS AYRTON: (following his blinking lead) Blink, blink.

PEEL: Blink, blink.

MRS AYRTON: Blink, blink.

(Lighting blinks to blackout in time with them)

12.

(When lighting comes in-tune-with-them blinkingly back on, PEEL is in a new shirt and waistcoat and she is in a new dress.

Off to the side, MACQUEEN is still 'chesting' away time-warped, even though MOCK has now gone.)

PEEL: (to her dress) New. Impressive.

MRS AYRTON: (to his new stuff) Same goes with your shirt.

PEEL: You pressed it.

MRS AYRTON: Underneath this very frock.

(They are embarrassed by the elegance of the exchange.

PEEL returns to being absorbed by coaxing 'his' sun to come back into the sky.

It seems the cue to release MACQUEEN who can now get out of his time-warp and can stride officiously in... so officiously, and so obviously there to 'take on' PEEL that he noticeably dares to step onto the piano without hesitation.

This, MRS AYRTON abruptly cuts off, moves defensively between the two men, arms crossed, except when almost absent-mindedly now slapping PEEL's 'automatic' groping attempts away, and...)

MACQUEEN: (re PEEL) Looks like he's sleeping.

MRS AYRTON: (protectively) He always looks like that when he's dead to the world. If you don't know that, you must be dead to the world.

MACQUEEN: Oh yeah, well what's he look like when he's really dead to the world?

MRS AYRTON: Dead asleep. Help you?

(MACQUEEN holds up handcuffs)

MACQUEEN: Come to collar him.

MRS AYRTON: ('oh yeah?') You've got a license for those things?

MACQUEEN: I've got a key. That's better than a license.

PEEL: Tick tock tick tock.

MRS AYRTON: He's sleeping.

MACQUEEN: ('gotcha') You said he was dead to the world!

MRS AYRTON: I might've and I might not've.
    (re handcuffs)
Give me one good reason.

MACQUEEN: He went n' maliciously wounded a native.

MRS AYRTON: How?

MACQUEEN: He injured the man's wrist parlously.

MRS AYRTON: How?

MACQUEEN: Way I hear of it was old Peel here…

MRS AYRTON: Who?

MACQUEEN: … Mr Peel here

MRS AYRTON: Who?

MACQUEEN: Commissariat Peel here turned his back when the fellow was trying to strike him with a waddy. Bounced off his shoulder blade, painful swelling of the wrist.

MRS AYRTON: What's a waddy when it's home?

MACQUEEN: A wooden club/stick thing.

MRS AYRTON: Somebody tried to hit him with a cricket bat?

MACQUEEN: Not a cricket bat, Madam.

MRS AYRTON: Sounds like a cricket bat to me.

MACQUEEN: Not that they have cricket bats here.

MRS AYRTON: Why not?

MACQUEEN: Don't really know. No cricket balls?

MRS AYRTON: I don't think you should be asking me. We are very careful with ours. Anyway, we were here all the time.

PEEL: Tick tock.

MACQUEEN: Missus, who else's goes around lookin' like he's got some tortoise shell or something on 'is back, but him?

MRS AYRTON: (on high horse) Whatnot.

MACQUEEN: Beggin' yours?

MRS AYRTON: Whatnot. He prefers whatnot, not something.

(She plants her feet more firmly, indicates PEEL)

MRS AYRTON: I said give me one good reason.

MACQUEEN: Why I'm here, like, over than that other reason?

MRS AYRTON: Why you're here, like.

MACQUEEN: (food for thought) Good point.

(then)
Might be how he mopes around with this sort of tortoise shell on his back like nothing can get through. Bad for the wrist behind any waddy, that.

MRS AYRTON: He does not mope around. I don't let him, not from behind, I don't.

MACQUEEN: Might be because people think he's hard and cruel all round.

MRS AYRTON: They do not.

MACQUEEN: How's about acrimonious and unscrupulous?

MRS AYRTON: 'Acrimonious' and 'scrupulous' haven't even entered the colony!

MACQUEEN: They have if you get a peek into Mock's book. How's about obstinate and mean?

MRS AYRTON: Poppycock!

MACQUEEN: Snobbish 'n snooty?

MRS AYRTON: Absolute tosh!

MACQUEEN: Blessed if I know then.

MRS AYRTON: Then your course is clear. You may leave the handcuffs but you must go.

MACQUEEN: (good compromise) Fair 'nough.

(and leaves the handcuffs and moves off.

134

*At the edge of the lighting, once again, he bumps into
MOCK coming in. They meet face-to-face and start
bouncing off each other again as though they time-
warped again and haven't stopped from last time)*

MRS AYRTON: Blink, blink.

PEEL: Blink, blink.

(and the lighting blinks on and off like a time strobe.

*When it returns, MACQUEEN has gone but MOCK,
now time-warped, is still bumping against him as though
he was still there.*

MOCK manages to stop, is confused)

MRS AYRTON: (at him) Now what do you want?

*(but MOCK has no idea why he is there, turns and
leaves.*

Alone with PEEL going distractedly…)

PEEL: Tick tock tick tock

*(… up at sky, she puts the handcuffs on herself and then
parades herself before PEEL as though modelling them
on her on a cat walk.*

*Certainly, his 'bad' arm shows a lot of interest,
especially when, encouraged by its grabbing
enthusiasms, she slips the gag back on and does a
terrible, yet still passable, imitation of the temptress
Salome.*

135

It is really only the quick onslaught of muscle fatigue that makes her stop and return to busying herself as normal about the place)

PEEL: Tick tock tick…

(Yet the fact is he is now more than halfway distracted by her now… and not just his arm.

It might be that she is deliberately bending over provocatively before him, or she might be innocent of such intention. However, he cannot take his eyes off her for long. He tries not to, tries to concentrate on enticing 'his' sun back, but his eyes are actually leading his 'bad' arm in shooting towards her amply parts.

The harder he tries to control himself, the more he begins to start twitching with the itches all over his body.

Each time he near reaches a grope of her, 'his' missing sun appears in electric flicker. It only encourages him, combines the possible rewards.

Finally, his whole torso follows his arm in one big uncontrollable lunge which just misses her, only because she has dodged-swivelled away at that point.

He cries out in alarm. She straightens because of it. It allows him to go back to his 'tick tock' cover-up but not before, realising what must have happened, she gives him one of her particularly-crushing sniggers that he is a failure.

There is a loud 'ahem' from off, and:)

FRED PEEL: Knock, knock.

(FRED is now dressed in the manner of a grandee of the medical profession – in full doublet and hose, cut-away coat, pin stripes, with an eminent doctor's Gladstone bag in his hand and a superior attitude in his bearing. Only the twinkle in his eye remains the same.

There is no doubt he has been watching the last danse macabre between his father and MRS AYRTON)

FRED PEEL: (without ado) Did I hear a cri de coeur from my old daddy?

MRS AYRTON: (at the bridgehead again) No disturbing. He's dead to the world.

(Nonetheless, FRED PEEL makes himself at home… noticeably a changed man… while nattering with her)

FRED PEEL: Not even to tell him I've become a proper doctor. Dr Frederic Peel says 'say aah'! I can even give him a middle finger if he likes. Not even then?

MRS AYRTON: No.

FRED PEEL: Not even if I could tell him I specialise in hard-ball injuries, especially to 12th men?

MRS AYRTON: Well… no. He's too busy.

FRED PEEL: Not even when it looks like he's out of The Master Plan?
    (PEEL stops his tick-tocking)
Hello, Granny.

MRS AYRTON: I ain't your granny. If I am, I deny it. And I said no disturbing.

FRED PEEL: Not even to tell him his unlawful son of me has made good and his daughter…yours… Dora's gone back to England and will only be coming back to marry his stable boy, now Chief Magistrate, whom he once only knew as Hall but now had better mind his p's and q's to, and his wife's run off with an unnamed whaling captain out of the original Perth and thereby cuckolded poor old Lieutenant Macqueen who cuckolded him, him being my one'n'only Poppa within touching distance…?
   (stops for breath)
Oh, and his new Residency's been preferred as a humpy for the whole local tribe who are learning the English word of 'thanks' from a one Mock who has become one of the richest merchants in the colony thanks to suddenly finding he is not understanding a word anyone's saying anymore.
   (and)
Not even then, Granny?

MRS AYRTON: He is at his new passion called astrology.

FRED PEEL: (nodding, sagely) Ah, passion. Well, it was lucky I was on the edge of the civilised world to hear'n'heed the medical emergency, Granny.

PEEL: (suddenly 'returning') My wife's up and left me. Somebody get her back. *I need a poke!*

FRED PEEL: There's my Poppa!
   (attends to him)
A poke like that might be a bit hard, Pops, since Mums been gone two years.

PEEL: Really?

(then, musing)
Her pokes weren't worth waiting dropping the strides for anyway. Never did once with her. Weren't bad pokes, though, far as pokes go.

FRED PEEL: Your divorce paved the way for my medical degree, Father, so ta.

PEEL: (dully) Tick tock. What's going on?
(adds his own reason)
Out laying the foundations on the rim of the world. Just fitting an over or two in, as it were. Far-flinging to the stars, what? You can yodel away but it don't get you no strudel. A batting man could find himself having to bat through the tea break.

MRS AYRTON: I don't care how many years it's been. They better not be talking gossip over any clothes line about him n' me.

(This is all satisfying to FRED PEEL who can now become doctor well and truly. He makes it onto the piano without anyone objecting, lays out his medical kit, and, to his father:)

FRED PEEL: Say 'got her'.

MRS AYRTON: He will not!

FRED PEEL: Now, Granny, I am here in my professional capacity.

MRS AYRTON: Yes, and that's how your mother came home with you.

FRED PEEL: (nevertheless) Say 'got her'.

PEEL: Gotcha.

FRED PEEL: No, 'got her'.

PEEL: Gotcha.

FRED PEEL: Try again?

PEEL: Gotcha.

FRED PEEL: Mmm, more serious than I thought. Now,
Father, I want you to think really carefully before you answer.

PEEL: (nodding) Thinking.

FRED PEEL: (indicating her) Do you really think deep down
in the depths of your arm you really want to?

PEEL: What?

FRED PEEL: Stoke the flames, fiddle with the fire…?

> *(PEEL sits stock still in shock for a moment. His son
> has to look closely to see tears running down his cheek
> and to gently wipe them away)*

FRED PEEL: There, there.

PEEL: (pathetically) Get their girds loined up. We're going
on the attack. Hit the Unknown for six. Barley's to singles.
Whack it over the fence.

FRED PEEL: (to soothe) Tick tock, if you want.

PEEL: Tick tock.

FRED PEEL: (kindly) I'd say it's a simple case of atrophied human congress. No pull for far too long. A condition – you are right -- of being poke-less.

MRS AYRTON: And whose fault is that?

    (PEEL grabs him, reels him in)

PEEL: You tell 'em all to come back. You tell 'em all I forgive 'em.

FRED PEEL: Well, see, Paps, they've either gone
    (points inland)
that way in one of Mock Esquire's first-class-for-the-uppercrust carriages, or gone
    (points out over the sea)
that way in one of Mock Esquire's first-class-for-the-uppercrust highfalutin' ships.

MRS AYRTON: Are you talking Mock as in Mock?

FRED PEEL: Ship, ferry, coach proprietor, purveyor of the best greasy wheels, gold miner, landlord. He's kickin' 'is heels outside to be let in right at this very minute.

PEEL: Mock, outside… is he sick?

FRED PEEL: He's become the owner of manners, Paps.

PEEL: What's the latest score?

FRED PEEL: The MCC's rep side is chasing the local Tribes by a fair margin. Didn't bring any spinners with 'em,

PEEL: I see.

(He makes a superhuman effort to rally, stands for her to brush him down)

PEEL: How's my back?

MRS AYRTON: Straight as a die. A tortoise would be proud of a back like that.

PEEL: Show Mock in.

(MRS AYRTON whistles very impressively with fingers and teeth.

MOCK, the grandee, enters with a flourish, tipping his toff's hat, poses waiting for applause, and:)

MOCK: (about himself) 'Ere, how's that for a transformation?

PEEL: (animated to see him) Mock! You found a way to make those roofs!

MOCK: Dunno about that, but I found a way to make more families. It's the same as making more customers.

PEEL: Don't be shy, Mock. All is forgiven!

MOCK: (cynic) Terrific.

PEEL: Sign a little contract renewal. New livery we'll dig around for or
    (re her pinafore dress)
use her pinny. It needs to come down a peg or two.

MOCK: (the merchant) Got a good feel to it, 'as it?

MRS AYRTON: (fronting MOCK) This ain't a servant's pinny.

MOCK: Alright, alright, keep your pinny on.

MRS AYRTON: My pinny is always on!

PEEL: (peacemaking) Mock!

MOCK: (alarmed) What!

PEEL: Did you get any education on the way? I always said: that Mock, he'd be good at education if you could take that brain of his and put a bit of putty into it.

MOCK: 'Ere, you'd be interested I'm going up to Oxford Uni next year, squire.

PEEL: Oh, how wonderful. It's a pity they won't let you in.

MOCK: At first, like. Until me legal eagles struck a deal for me paying to being one of Sir Joseph Banks's specimens by night and a student by day.

PEEL: My God, they've got lawyers here now?

MOCK: (nodding) All's going to the dingoes, squire.

PEEL: (proudly to her) Native dogs. See, that's the interpreter training I gave him.

MOCK: No, it weren't.

PEEL: Yes, it were't.

MACK: No, it weren't.

143

PEEL: Yes, it…
(stops the roundabouting, chuckles)
See how skillful in debating I made him? My Mock.

MOCK: 'Ere, nice to be pleasant, squire, but you're squattin'
away on my land, that's the thing.

FRED PEEL: (as shocked as all) Steady, Mock. He's not as
young as he used to be.

MOCK: (fairly guilty) I just come to collect me rent.

FRED PEEL: You agreed to an acorn a year quit rent.

MOCK: (getting hot under the collar) None of my mob know
what an acorn even looks like. Next you'll be goin' on about
makin' it a local peppercorn? Oh, no, matey. That's culture
wars right there, that is.

PEEL: Please, old chap…

MOCK: (not to be stopped) You laying around and goin'
swimming on me land. My mob want a bit of layin' around
and goin' swimming.

FRED PEEL: What would you want to go and do that for?

MOCK: We want to get washed up on the beach, run out an'
get washed back in again too. Why do youse all get the luxury
of lookin' stupid?

FRED PEEL: (understanding, sadly) You want your bums bit
off too.

MOCK: We got the right to come out from the shade, sit on

144

our own beach an' open an umbrella for a little shade. 'Ere, it ain't like your fleas versus our fleas. Them's our sand flies! Culture don't only come with English.

FRED PEEL: That doesn't make sense, Mock.

MOCK: If we wanted to make sense, we'd stick to our own culture, see.
(repents anger, mutters)
Make it a peppercorn, so I can't stay mad at yer.

PEEL: (again) Mock!

MOCK: (alarmed) What?!

(PEEL, now looking old, shows real open rebellion to her, to his situation)

PEEL: Look what you left me with.

MRS AYRTON: Hey!

(MOCK goes to PEEL, as though recognising the old man coming out in him, holds his head for a moment)

MOCK: She's got some gold in 'er teeth. Don't throw it away lightly, squire.

(He paternally pats PEEL's cheek, then leaves, not without reluctance of leaving PEEL behind.

To console him, FRED PEEL also goes to his father – it being noticeable that the piano area is no longer taboo – and actually has to bend over to hear him)

PEEL: I'll show 'em.

FRED PEEL: How, Father?

PEEL: With one hand tied behind me back.

FRED PEEL: (but kindly) With one arm strapped down? How's that?

PEEL: (great umpiring call) Not out!

FRED PEEL: That's the ticket.

PEEL: How'd I go in my benefit match?

FRED PEEL: Very good! You made the eleven!

PEEL: 'Bout bloody time. Any peerage?

FRED PEEL: No peerage.

PEEL: They keep digging up the pitch.

FRED PEEL: They found a lot of gold down there, that's why. Well, Mock did.

PEEL: (up to empty sky) Tick tock.

FRED PEEL: That's it.

PEEL: Tick tock.

> (Gesturing, the doctor tries to get MRS AYRTON to take over from him, but she shuns this, turns, bends over ostensibly at chores.

> At the ample sight she presents, FRED PEEL shudders,

while PEEL's arm fights to get free)

FRED PEEL: (still carl-kindly) Papa?
  (and)
What we have to guard against medically-speaking is thinking
that that arm of yours, with that shoulder of yours and that
hand of yours is… you know… capable of a *meaningful act.*

PEEL: (dully) Is that what's it's coming to?

FRED PEEL: I don't know, Father. But I think your arm
does, you see.

> *(He pats his father on the head and ostensibly leaves,
> kissing MRS AYRTON's hand as he goes. Yet we notice
> he stands to the side, essentially not quite 'off',
> observing.)*

MRS AYRTON: Blink.

PEEL: (following suit) Blink.

> *(A quick blackout, then, literally in the blink of an eye…)*

13.
(PEEL and MRS AYRTON are in the same positions.

*FRED PEEL can just be made out standing in the
shadows off to one side.*

*At first, PEEL remains sitting and forlornly gazing up to
where 'his' missing sun should be.*

147

Then he nods, as though receiving an idea, nods, gets to his feet, removes the arm sling and approaches MRS AYRTON, who, either deliberately or not, is bending over amply before him.

He advances on her.

This is done in extreme slow motion, with his hand and then his arm and then his shoulder excruciatingly reaching out towards her, as though it was independent of him and being manipulated by puppetry.

PEEL himself seems to be moving through syrup, swimming against a physical presence.

As he does so, FRED PEEL, the doctor, does a commentary on the arm's progress and does so in monotone:)

FRED PEEL: One, the shoulder. The point of the shoulder is drawn forward by the action of the serratus superior and pectorals. Rotation of the scapula, when the arm is raised, s effected by the trapezius and serratus anterior. Two, the ar. The triceps act directly as an extensor of the elbow joint. The long head of the muscle undergoes passive stretching. The biceps flex the forearm, passing over the head of the humerus and preventing a tendency of upwards displacement when downwards pressure is effected by the hand. Three, the hand. The flexor and extensor muscles when acting together produce adduction and abduction respectively at the wrist and the intercarpal joints, drawing the thumb forward in a plane at right angle to the palm. Note how the tendons and the small muscles are indispensable to the finer movements of the thenar eminence and digiti minini, called…
(kept back for exact timing)
opposition.

(PEEL's hand is now poised just above her lower rump, is now crabbing to make its grab)

FRED PEEL: Somewhere beneath all this lies the man.

(Finally, PEEL's hand makes its desperate move. It lunges down and grabs a handful of MRS AYRTON's lower band)

PEEL: BINGO!

(In triumphant he points with his 'good' arm up into the sky where 'his' sun has burst back into all its glorious light. And remains triumphant over all while she hops around outraged and PEEL hangs tigerishly on)

MRS AYRTON: MURDER! RAPE! GRABBED!

(But a smile comes on her face, and her dancing around takes on a flit by one of the ecstatic swans from 'Swan Lake'. A little giggle breaks out among her screams.

Blackout)

14.

(MRS AYRTON is spread-eagled on the piano top, with her legs open and her petticoats hoisted suggestively.

PEEL is sitting defeated, but at least he has 'his' sun back and so can be alone and defiant if need be.

'His' sun is sliding quite nicely and normally from east

149

to west and returning in the west now. We can perhaps hear PEEL softly chanting 'tick tock' in time with its passages.

MACQUEEN enters. MRS AYRTON guiltily gets to her feet to confront him, to guard PEEL. It takes a lot of effort)

MACQUEEN: I left those handcuffs behind.

(She actually has them to hand but is cagey about having to hand them back)

MRS AYRTON: What handcuffs?

(But he sees that she knows something. He moves closer to raise his eyebrows and nod towards PEEL. She won't confirm)

MACQUEEN: (to PEEL) I say, Peel, the handcuffs I left?
    (gets very little response)
If you don't give them back, old son, I can't nick you, can I?.

MRS AYRTON: (producing them) These?

(He goes to take them back with pretended surprise, but virtually has to snatch them off her.)

MACQUEEN: Hold out your hands.

(She does)

MACQUEEN: Not you.
    (back at PEEL)
Let's 'ave you, Thomas Peel.

*(She puts out her wrists again. It is an automatic
reaction, which he sees and amuses himself a few times
in producing it from her by pushing the handcuffs
towards PEEL.*

*And, anyway, he can see by waving his hand in front of
PEEL that there is no likelihood of escape)*

MRS AYRTON: Leave him alone!

MACQUEEN: 'Ere, it was you who cried out 'Rape'.

MRS AYRTON: (correcting) 'Wolf'.

MACQUEEN: 'Rape'.

MRS AYRTON: 'Wolf'.

MACQUEEN: All right, Mr Thomas Peel, I hereby arrest you
on the charge of 'Wolf'.
    (and, anyway, straightens quickly)
Attenshun!

*(In strides HALL now judge-attired and very officially.
The others straggle behind him, but in some sort of
courtly order)*

HALL: Right, the court is standing!

*(He sits and then has to stand by his own order. He
raises his gavel, then points it at PEEL)*

HALL: I said the court is *standing*.
    (to MACQUEEN's confusion)
That means he must take a *stance*, man.

151

*(PEEL readily nods, gets up and takes up a cricketing
stance at the crease on the piano. But MACQUEEN
dutifully guides him to stand before the now Chief
Magistrate, forcing him by nudge to come alive,
somewhat, to his surroundings)*

PEEL: Hall…?

MACQUEEN: Your Honour to you, Peel.

PEEL: Hall of fame?

MACQUEEN: You just shut it an' wait until you see what he
says about that.

HALL: (proclaiming) Stand up for the petty sessions. Stand
still. Stand aside. All standing? Who rang the bell?

MACQUEEN: He rang her. That's what we're here for.

HALL: Everybody knows that. What we are here today is to
find out could something like that be possible?

PEEL: (absent-mindedly) Whatnot.

HALL: (standing corrected) … could something whatnot like
that be possible.

MACQUEEN: (shaking head) Hard to believe.

MRS AYRTON: Hey!

HALL: We are not here to find out about that, as hard to
believe as it might be. We are here, I believe, to unfind the
find or I'd even entertain the other way around.

152

(in the silence which has to follow that:)

PEEL: Hall? My stable hand?

HALL: Do we have the first witness?

PEEL: Me son-in-law what shovelled shit?

MACQUEEN: Good point, that.
(at HALL)
Shouldn't you be excusing yourself or som'thing?

MRS AYRTON: (correcting) Whatnot.

MACQUEEN: (complying) Or whatnot.

HALL: (stroking chin) I could, I could. But we have already
established it's the whatnot of the thing. So, I be not excused.
Also, how many judges are there in the colony who have been
made to shovel shit by such a wicked felon of a father-in-law
like him?

FRED PEEL: Bit pre-judging, ain't it?

HALL: Of course it is! Good Lord, fellow, are we here or not
here?
(then to MACQUEEN)
And if there are no other judges with a wicked felon of a
father-in-law like I have, who is qualified to replace me by
being better able to shovel shit?
(MACQUEEN can only shrug dunno)
What is the charge?

MACQUEEN: Clutch-ery.

HALL: By the heavens, clutch-ery! I like a good evil grope-
153

ery! If there is not order in the court, there will be standing orders! Who else has to bring down the Rod of Aaron upon his pervert of a father-in-law coming the cop-this-lot on his mother-in-law? Unprecedented! A firstie! You may talk about unique, but I certainly will!
(and)
Bring in the first witness!

(There seems to be no first witness)

HALL: Tell that wife of mine to get in here and don't forget to read the notes I gave her word-for-word.

(DORA enters, the perfect judge's wife. She crosses to her grandmother, briefly lays her head on her bosom by way of embrace, then turns towards the 'court'…)

PEEL: Dora? My Dorie?

HALL: Quiet in the sixpennies!
(and)
Complete the disgusting charge.

MACQUEEN: This 'ere defendant did commit the 'orrible offence upon the person of his 'ousekeeper which we are here to find could be believable in this day'n'age.

HALL: Too true.

MACQUEEN: … causing her to make things look even worse like in disturbing the peace at a time of native uprisings requiring bloody murder elsewhere. According to the medical opinion of Dr Frederic Peel, one of the colony, this 'ere's shoulder egged on 'is arm which egged on 'is hand to you-know-what belonging to this 'ere lady.

154

VOICE OFF: Did someone say 'lady'?

HALL: And what does the first witness say?

DORA: Sand flies are absolute cannibals in this part of the Empire. *Cannibals.*

HALL: The matter at hand, Mrs Hall.

DORA: All I can say in defense of my father because I am a bit dim is when I heard it I couldn't believe it. And you may include the sand flies in that.

HALL: ('step down') Thank you. All right, second witness, which I believe makes it my turn next.
    (and pronouncing)
He, being related to me by an accidental shot in my own foot approximate to an altar the termites had gotten to last time I looked…

    (stops. All wait for more but that is all)

HALL: The third witness, please.

FRED PEEL: (stepping forward) What can I say?

    (Again, they wait for more, but he shrugs:)

FRED PEEL: Hey, it was a rhetorical question.

HALL: Next witness.

    (MRS AYRTON steps forward boldly. Obviously defending her PEEL, she holds up her gag and wrist-rope and casts them from her. She goes to speak but is cut off by)

155

HALL: Merely turn around please, madam.

(With his finger to his lips for silence, he motions for a twirl from her and after she has done so perplexed, he motions for her to do so again. These are, of course, twirl full of rump.

He gestures for her to be led back to near PEEL)

HALL: I think that adequately goes to the question whether is there anyone of whatnot status who still can't believe it?
    (and)
I think not
    (and)
Next. Ah, Mr Mock.

(MOCK comes forward from the shadows)

MOCK: I called this gentleman 'mighty sir' and won't deny it. 'Ere's the thing, to my mind… he never took up much room.

(steps back.

HALL dusts his hands off)

HALL: Mr Thomas Peel, we cannot overlook the distress of this fortunate woman…

MACQUEEN: (whispered correction) Unfortunate wo…

HALL: … of this *very* fortunate woman and your obvious inability to lay down any sort of decent innings that helped your side. Even the drink's trays rattled scandalously.
    (he hears PEEL mutter something)

What was that?

MRS AYRTON: (to his defense) He said he was found only just out of his ground.

HALL: (carrying on judgment) Mr Thomas Peel Esquire, you are bound over to be of reputable character for all of the foreseeable future and fined fifty pounds, which will come in handy albeit a stain of all our characters for how it will certainly come in handy. And frankly saying...

(But, despite all expectation, he has finished.

He departs grandly and the others follow, even though FRED PEEL lingers a bit.

After they are quite gone, PEEL musters up, yet weakly:)

PEEL: Bounders! Kangaroo court!

MRS AYRTON: Ssh, Mr Peel.

(She leads him back to the piano, gets him seated before 'his' sun, which is now shining brightly and moving perfectly-fitly.

He is putty in her hands.

She sits down beside him, puts a loving arm around him.

When his arm retaliates by sneakily edging towards her bum, she takes it gently and guides it up to be around her waist.

They sit 'in' the sun, side-by-side, arms around each other, and do not, nor need to, move.)

MRS AYRTON: Tomorrow we'll start digging for those piano keys.

(Blackout)

After the final curtain...

For one whole year, he had seemed paralysed and utterly incapable of moving even from the beach he landed on, while on another beach his people had been dying of starvation, scurvy, dysentery and exposure.

Finally, his people had had to desert him as quite mad.

His wife and daughter had also deserted him, leaving him saddled with his mother-in-law and his wife's love child. For thirty-six years, he stood a lonely, haughty and solitary figure blinded to his failings.

Eventually, at old age, he suffered the indignity of being brought before the magistrate for some decrepit and unspecified sexual misconduct against his haggard housekeeper, but the more rumour-mill slant was it was more against his mother-in-law, Mrs Ayrton, whom it seems he never fated to escape.

There is a commemorative headstone at Mandurah, Perth, for him. According to this, he was buried on top of his mother-in-law, who is 'chiselled' on that very same headstone. It doesn't seem to be any kind of joke, unfortunately.

However, it is fair to say…
(the Dictionary of Australian Biography, Percival Serle:)
'As he grew older and poorer and crustier, and more withdrawn, he became a legend. Clad in a faded red hunting coat, he was often to be seen riding alone through the bush in his large domain. Governor Stirling and the first settlers had always given him the respect due to one who had made an immense attempt to aid in the foundation of the colony and whose failure was partly due to a series of unfortunate circumstances. His character has often been blamed for this

failure, and it is true that he was hot-tempered, proud and often intolerant of stupidity. On the other hand, he had vision, courage and strict standards of behaviour: almost unique among the early settlers, he never complained either about the country or his ill fortune. As one of his contemporaries and equals said, he 'displayed singular fortitude considering the severe losses he had sustained'.

Peel died at Mandurah on 22 December 1865 and was buried in the churchyard there.

Out of the original 250,000 acres or 1000 square kilometres he had eventually been granted, he left an estate of shares in a company which he had traded for his remaining 107,000 acres that he had left. He divided his estate between his son, his daughter and his reputed son.'

---oOo---